DOCTOR ON BOARD

DOCTOR ON BOARD

Your Practical Guide to Medical Emergencies at Sea

Dr J Hauert

verified by Shelley Johnson

SHERIDAN HOUSE

This edition first published 2010 by
Sheridan House Inc.
145 Palisade Street
Dobbs Ferry, NY 10522
www.sheridanhouse.com

First published in Germany
under the title *Medizinischer Ratgeber an Bord*
by Delius Klasing Verlag

A CIP catalog record for this book is available from the Library of Congress,
Washington, DC
This book is produced using paper that is made from wood grown in managed,
sustainable forests. It is natural, renewable and recyclable. The logging and
manufacturing processes conform to the environmental regulations of the
country of origin.

U.S. edition edited by Janine Simon
First Aid Kit © by Ed Mapes

Note: while all reasonable care has been taken in the publication of this book,
the publisher takes no responsibility for the use of the methods or products
described in the book.

ISBN 978-1-57409-298-1

Printed and bound in China by C&C Offset Printing Co

CONTENTS

FOREWORD

Sailing should be exciting and challenging enough without the added drama of a medical emergency on board. But if someone is injured or falls ill at sea, where help is not always close by, it's important for a skipper and other crew members to be equipped with the knowledge and skills that could prove lifesaving.

Aiming to go beyond simply first aid, this book describes what to do in the event of near-drowning, sudden unconsciousness, choking and bleeding, and details how to treat cuts, breakages, fractures and dislocations, as well as more common problems like burns, seasickness and muscle strain. It also covers serious medical situations that could arise because of extreme heat and cold, and less common emergencies involving infections, poisoning, and bites and stings which can spoil a voyage. The book also gives practical advice about nutrition, hygiene and immunisation. It's the full package!

Of course, seeking professional advice is recommended in any situation but this book assumes this has not been possible. When you don't have a doctor on board, and have only your own resources to rely upon, the advice given here could prove to be the difference between life and death.

USEFUL ADDRESSES:

The Department of State offers medical advice to travelers
Website: www.travel.state.gov

The U.S. Coast Guard will get you in touch with a local hospital and with CIRM, a worldwide medical consulting organization.
Website: www.uscgboating.org

Centers for Disease Control and Prevention (CDC) will provide a wealth of information on various topics
Tel. 1-800-311-3435
Emergency number: 1-800-232-4636
Website: www.cdc.gov/

CDC provides also information about Certificates of Vaccination and health topics for travelers.
Tel. 1-877-394-8747
Website: www.cdc.gov/travel/

The American Association of Poison Control Centers operates an emergency hotline:
1-800-222-1222

The International Association for Medical Assistance to Travelers (IAMAT) gives valuable information on the risk of diseases and a list of English-speaking physicians around the world.
IAMAT
Tel. 1-716-754-4883
Website: www.iamat.org.

FIRST AID ON BOARD

It is difficult for any crew member with a non-medical background to assess an accident or illness correctly. This is why it is vital that at least one, preferably two crew members, have attended a comprehensive first aid course, and are confident in first aid techniques, including resuscitation and minor surgical procedures such as stitching wounds. Indeed, if you are on an extended cruise and are faced with a traumatic injury far from land – and help – then prompt and correct treatment of the patient by other crew members will be essential.

The aims of the first aider should be to:
- Remove the casualty from further harm to a safe place (eg if the cause of the incident is from toxic gases, smoke, fire, electrical shock etc).
- Assess the casualty's ABC status (see below).
- Control bleeding (see page 15).
- Treat for shock if necessary (see page 20).

THE UNCONSCIOUS CASUALTY
If the patient is suffering from respiratory failure or cardiac arrest, **Cardiopulmonary Resuscitation (CPR)** treatment should be given without delay to avoid permanent injury or death.

THE ABC RESUSCITATION RULE
ABC stands for **A**IRWAY, **B**REATHING, **C**IRCULATION/**C**OMPRESSION
If the casualty is unconscious or does not respond immediately, open their airway and check their breathing. If the casualty is breathing, place in the recovery position (see Fig 5). Keep checking that the airway remains clear, and continue to monitor the casualty.

If they are not breathing:
- Lie the casualty on their back, lift the chin with two fingers and gently tilt the head back to open the airway (see Figs 2 and 3). Sometimes this is sufficient to get the breathing started so check for breathing again by looking for chest movement, listening and feeling for exhaled air (see Fig 1).

Fig 1 Check for exhaled air.

- You don't need to clear the casualty's mouth unless you can clearly see something in there such as seaweed or food.
- When checking for breathing, look, listen and feel for no more than 10 seconds. If the patient is still not breathing normally, commence chest compressions without delay.

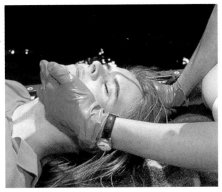

Fig 2 Extend the head and neck to clear the airway.

RESCUE BREATHING

- Open the airway (tilt head and lift chin), pinch the nostrils and give two 'rescue breaths' (mouth-to-mouth), taking one second for each breath and ensuring that the chest rises and falls (see Fig 4).
- If the rescue breaths do not make the chest rise and fall, recheck that the airway is open and remove any visible obstructions and that their mouth is completely sealed by yours.
- Carry on continuous cycles of chest compressions and rescue breaths (ratio 30:2) until a) qualified help arrives and takes over, b) casualty starts breathing spontaneously or c) you become exhausted.
- If another first aider is present, they should take over CPR after 2 minutes or so to prevent fatigue.
- If the casualty starts to breathe spontaneously, place the casualty in the recovery position and continue to monitor closely.
- Summon emergency medical assistance by radio or phone, at first opportunity.

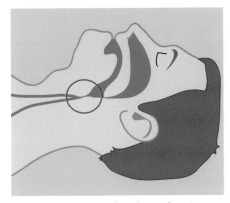
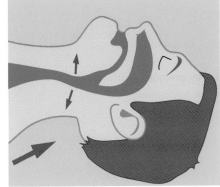

Fig 3 Extend the neck to keep the airway open (see also Fig 2).
Left: blocked airway, right: open airway.

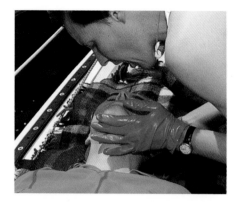

◀ **Fig 4 Mouth-to-mouth rescue breathing – make sure there is a complete seal over the mouth.**

Where possible, the use of resuscitation aids such as a pocket face mask or plastic face shield will minimise cross-infection and prevent secretions from the casualty reaching the rescuer.

As an alternative to mouth-to-mouth resuscitation, mouth-to-nose resuscitation is equally effective. Where there is damage to the mouth or teeth or an obstruction present, mouth-to-nose breathing is the preferred technique.

■ Release the casualty's nose and close his mouth (see Fig 6).
■ Seal your mouth around the nose and blow in steadily as for the mouth-to-mouth technique
■ Allow the mouth to open to let the breath out.

Fig 5 Recovery (coma) position.

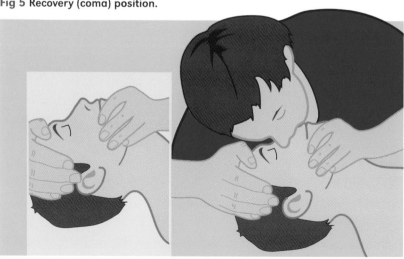

Fig 6 Mouth-to-nose rescue breathing.

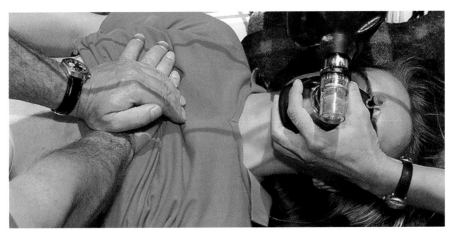

Fig 7 Cardiac massage and rescue breathing, here shown with a bag valve mask, known as an Ambu bag.

CHEST COMPRESSIONS _____

■ Kneel alongside the patient and place both interlocked hands in the centre of the chest (not on the ribs or the bottom of the breast bone), and press down with the heel of the hand.

■ Give 30 chest compressions at a rate of 100 per minute (see Fig 8). Press down on the breastbone approximately 4–5 cm. Allow the chest to come completely back up after each compression.

▶ Fig 8 Give cardiac compressions to the centre of the chest – 30 compressions to 2 rescue breaths.

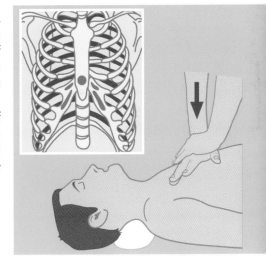

CHOKING: ADULTS

If the larynx is blocked by a foreign body and the victim is gasping for air but still able to talk, encourage the casualty to cough. If this does not relieve the obstruction, give him up to five strong blows between the shoulder blades, supporting his chest with one of your hands.

If the five back blows don't work, try abdominal thrusts (the Heimlich manoeuvre, see Fig 9):

■ Stand behind the person who is choking.

- Put your arms around their stomach.
- Make a fist and grab your fist with your other hand.
- Position the fist on the abdomen, just above the navel.
- Pull inwards and upwards up to five times.
- Check in the mouth again to see if the object has become dislodged.
- If at any stage the person becomes unconscious, you must start CPR.

Fig 9 Abdominal thrusts – for a choking casualty.

CHOKING: INFANTS AND CHILDREN

If the child is coughing effectively, no external manoeuvre is necessary. Continue to monitor the child carefully and encourage coughing to relieve the obstruction.
If the child is still conscious but not coughing effectively, give back blows:

FOR AN INFANT LESS THAN ONE YEAR

- Lay the infant face down on your lap with the head supported and lowermost.
- Deliver up to 5 sharp back blows with the heel of one hand in the middle of the back between the shoulder blades.
- If back blows do not relieve the obstruction, lay the infant on his back along your arm with his head down, supporting his head with your hand.
- Give up to 5 chest thrusts on the lower breastbone using 2 fingers of one hand. These are similar to chest compressions but sharper and slower.

FOR A CHILD OVER ONE YEAR

- Try to position the child on your lap with the head down. If this is not possible, lean the child forward and deliver the back blows from behind. Give up to 5 sharp back blows between the shoulder blades.
- Check the mouth following back blows to see if the obstruction is visible.
- If back blows do not relieve the obstruction, encircle your arms around the child from behind.
- Give up to 5 abdominal thrusts, between the navel and the bottom of the breastbone, using a clenched fist and a sharp, inward and upward movement.

SEVERE BLEEDING

SEVERE EXTERNAL BLEEDING

Severe loss of blood is life-threatening. The human body contains on average 5 litres (ca. 5 quarts) of blood, and signs of shock will occur after the loss of 1 to 2 litres (ca. 1 to 2 quarts). The amount of external bleeding tends to be overestimated by first aiders rather than underestimated.

Internal bleeding caused by blunt injuries to the abdomen or chest are dangerous as they are not obvious. If a serious injury has occurred, for instance, due to a fall from the mast or from a cable snapping, you must first determine the degree of seriousness of the injury.

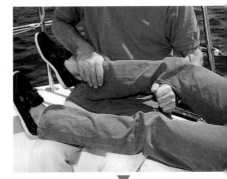

TREATMENT

■ Apply direct pressure to the wound with a sterile pad or compression bandage (see Fig 11) or any clean material if pad and pressure bandage are not immediately available. Wear gloves. Check there are no embedded objects in the wound, such as broken glass, before applying direct pressure.

■ Raise and support the injured limb, taking extra care if you suspect a bone has been broken. Lay the casualty down to treat for shock (see page 20). If possible, bandage the pad or dressing to control bleeding but not so tightly that it stops the circulation to fingers or toes. If bleeding seeps through the first bandage, cover with a second bandage. If bleeding continues to seep through the bandage, remove it and reapply.

■ Check mobility and sensation of the limb below the bleeding point to ensure good circulation (see Fig 10).

Fig 10 Check mobility by asking the casualty to push against something – compare one side of the body with the other.

■ If the casualty is complaining of tingling or numbness in the affected limb, the bandage may be too tight. The fingers or toes may also feel cool or look pale. Circulation can be checked by firmly pressing on the casualty's fingernail bed and then releasing the pressure. The pink colour should return to the nail bed within 1–2 seconds. A delay could indicate impairment of the circulation. The pulse below the wound should also be checked (see Fig 18).

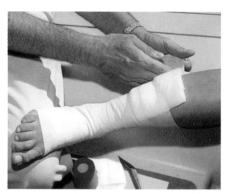

Fig 11 Apply a compression bandage for severe bleeding.

■ Dirty wounds should be cleaned with an antiseptic (see Fig 12). The most effective way to clean a dirty wound is by irrigating it with a large syringe filled with sterile water or saline solution. In the case of injuries to limbs, you should also immobilise the leg or arm with any suitable material to hand (see Fig 13). Care should be taken to cushion the limb.

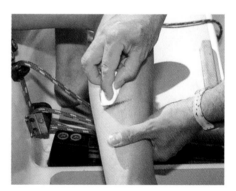

Fig 12 Clean wounds with antiseptic.

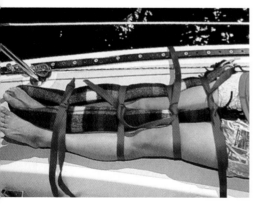

Fig 13 Immobilising an injured leg with a blanket and webbing.

Fig 14 Transfer the injured person to the cabin and make sure they are both comfortable and safe.

■ Remove the casualty to a safe, quiet place (see Fig 14).

■ For chest and open abdominal injuries, the same procedure of applying a sterile covering and immobilisation should be followed (see Fig 15).

■ Only in extremely rare cases, for instance, rupture of the femoral artery, is it necessary to apply pressure to the blood vessel. The appropriate pressure points are shown in Fig 18.

■ If bleeding soaks through initial dressing, leave in place and add second clean dry dressing on top. Continue to apply direct pressure over bleeding site.

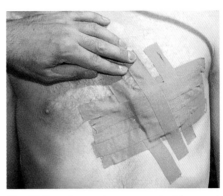

Fig 15 Treating a chest wound with a pad taped to the body.

▼ Fig 16 Application of a splint to the lower arm and a bandage to hold the splint in place.

INTERNAL BLEEDING

Severe blows to the body causing internal bleeding are particularly dangerous and difficult for the first aider to recognise. They mostly manifest themselves only through the subsequent shock symptoms (low blood pressure, high pulse rate, paleness, confusion). Any violent blow to the costal arch (the bottom of the rib cage) or the abdomen can lead to internal bleeding.

TREATMENT _____

■ The casualty must be kept under constant observation and outside medical aid summoned immediately.

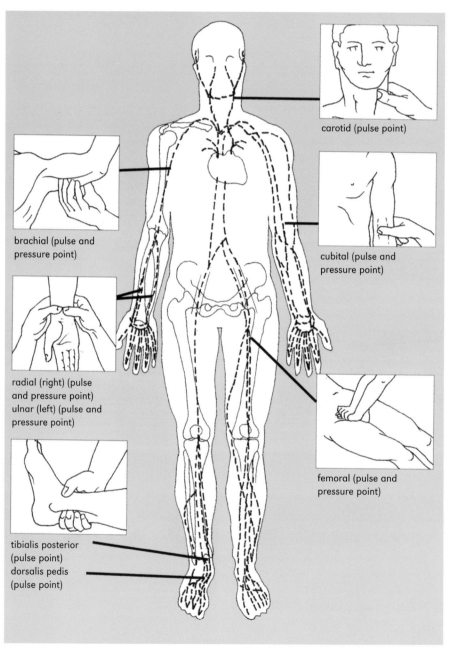

carotid (pulse point)

brachial (pulse and
pressure point)

cubital (pulse and
pressure point)

radial (right) (pulse
and pressure point)
ulnar (left) (pulse and
pressure point)

femoral (pulse and
pressure point)

tibialis posterior
(pulse point)
dorsalis pedis
(pulse point)

Fig 18 Pulse points and pressure points.

■ Carefully feel the abdomen (see Fig 19), in order to determine which area is the most painful. Check for swelling. If the casualty needs to be evacuated, a horizontal, stable, lying position with knees bent is recommended. Do not allow the casualty to have anything to eat or drink, except sips of water to wet the mouth.

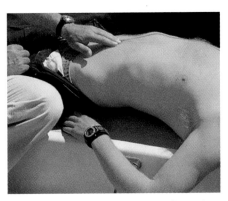

Fig 19 Gently feel the abdomen for pain and swelling.

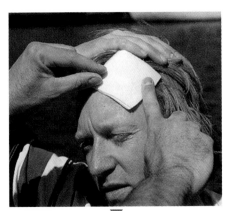

■ In the case of external head injuries, the first thing to do is to stop the blood flow using a sterile pad and bandage (see Fig 20). It is important to monitor the casualty's state of consciousness.

Fig 20 A sterile pad and compression bandage being applied to a lacerated head wound. A triangular bandage is used to cover the head.

SHOCK

During shock, vital bodily functions are reduced as blood flow is redirected away from the skin to the vital organs. Nearly all injuries can cause shock; particularly bleeding, extensive burns, the fracture of major bones with blood loss and other severe injuries accompanied by extreme pain. Similarly, allergic reactions, inhalation of gases and chemical substances, bleeding of internal organs, as well as peritonitis, heart attack, brain injuries, spinal injuries and metabolic disorders such as diabetes, can trigger shock.

Symptoms include the skin being pale, cool and usually clammy. Breathing is shallow and rapid, the pulse is weak and rapid, possibly also irregular (pulse rate above 100), and blood pressure drops. The casualty complains of thirst, nausea and may vomit. Psychological signs may include restlessness, agitation, anxiety but also apathy.

TREATMENT

- If possible, remove the cause of shock and deal with any bleeding.
- Ensure the airways are clear as per the ABC rule on page 10.
- Make the casualty comfortable and provide plenty of reassurance.
- If the casualty is conscious, lay him flat, with the legs slightly raised (see Fig 22).
- In the event of head injuries or breathing difficulties, keep the torso raised (see Fig 21).
- If the casualty is semi-conscious or unconscious, place in the recovery position (see Fig 23).
- The casualty should be kept warm using blankets, but should not be actively warmed up, as this would worsen their circulation.

Fig 21 For a head injury or breathing difficulties, place the patient in this position – torso raised and legs lowered.

Fig 22 This is the best position for a shock casualty – keep the legs raised.

Fig 23 The recovery position – place the patient on cushions on the floor if possible.

- If severe pain is the cause of shock, give painkillers in sufficient quantity (see First Aid Kit, page 92). Take care if blood pressure is already very low.
- Do not give the patient anything to drink but moisten lips with liquid.
- If the cause of shock is found to be loss of fluids due to repeated vomiting, diarrhoea or extensive burns, a conscious casualty can be given an electrolytic drink.
- In the case of life-threatening allergic shock (anaphylaxis), immediately administer adrenaline if you carry this on board and know how to administer it (see page 92).
- Afterwards continue treatment with cortisone (or antihistamine) tablets. In most cases, the individuals affected are aware of their allergic predisposition (animals, nuts, bee stings etc), and are properly prepared.
- Adrenaline is available as an auto-injector which is administered by the casualty himself or by the first aider (if instructed on use in case of emergency)

Fig 24 These two pairs of photographs show ways of removing the casualty from the danger zone.

■ As it is usually impossible for the first aider to find the real cause of shock, outside medical advice should be sought by radio.

■ Pulse, blood pressure (use digital battery operated apparatus if you don't know how to take blood pressure), respiration and the level of response from the casualty must be constantly monitored until the medical help arrives.

SEIZURES, EPILEPSY, HYPERVENTILATION, AGITATION, ALCOHOL WITHDRAWAL

All of these conditions often appear to the first aider to be signs of shock. A full examination is required to ascertain the underlying cause.

EPILEPSY

Epileptic fits are caused by abnormal brain activity. Psychological and physical stress may trigger fits, however, the person may have simply forgotten to take their anti-epileptic tablets regularly, since they are out of their normal routine. The individual will feel discomfort and will usually be aware of his impending situation. They can warn fellow sailors to whom an attack of this type seems extremely alarming.

The seizures then follow, usually with muscle contractions and convulsions. The danger is that the individual may cause himself harm, particularly in the confined space on board. Sometimes there is involuntary loss of control of bladder and bowels. The convulsions generally pass within a few minutes and after this, the individual falls into a drowsy state. The individual will have no recollection of the event.

TREATMENT

Injuries can mostly be avoided if the epileptic patient is handled correctly.

- Don't put anything in the person's mouth, including your fingers as this could cause more damage. They might bite their tongue but this will heal.
- Put something soft under the person's head.
- Only move the person if they are in a dangerous place on the boat. If you do transfer them, ensure there is adequate cushioning (see Fig 25).
- Move things away from them if there is a risk of injury.
- Do not attempt to restrain the convulsive movements.
- Put into recovery position after the fit if the person is not fully conscious, and stay with them.
- Advise the casualty to see a doctor if it is the first time they have had a seizure.

Normally, an epileptic fit will subside within a few minutes, but if the person is having continuous fits or if a fit lasts longer than 10 minutes, it may be necessary to administer an anti-epileptic medication such as Diazepam liquid (10mg), rectally.

Fig 25 Transfer the epileptic to a safe place with adequate cushioning – monitor them carefully.

HYPERVENTILATION

Hyperventilation syndrome is an excessive increase in respiration. The sufferer becomes agitated and begins to breathe in quickly and deeply. This causes a lack of calcium in the blood. The sufferer seems over-anxious, agitated and complains of numbness or tingling in hands and feet. He or she may faint. Anxiety is the most common cause of hyperventilation – the sufferer may be experiencing a panic attack. The symptoms usually last between 20 to 30 minutes.

TREATMENT

- The cycle of anxiety, irregular respiration and increasing nervousness must be broken by a crew member calming the sufferer.
- Try to engage in conversation with the person and get them to focus on particular objects.
- If you cannot manage to get the patient to return to breathing normally by calming him, try getting him to re-breathe his exhaled air out of a plastic bag.

STATES OF AGITATION

Symptoms similar to those of hyperventilation may also be found in sensitive individuals who are stressed by conditions on board. Members of crew with definite psychiatric disorders such as schizophrenia and depression should consult their doctor before embarking on a lengthy sailing trip, and obtain appropriate written advice for any emergency which might arise. They should give full details to the skipper when they go on board.

The possibilities for therapy on board a boat are obviously limited. However a calm and caring attitude on the part of the skipper and other members of crew will be of great benefit to the sufferer.

TREATMENT

■ In the event of evident psychotic episodes (thoughts of suicide, altered perception, hallucinations), do not hesitate to get outside advice via the radio.
■ The individual should not be left alone under any circumstances.
■ The sufferer should carry their own supply of anti-psychotic medications but failing that, medicinal therapy may be attempted with Diazepam (anti-anxiety medication) and Chlorpromazine (Thorazine, anti-psychosis medication), if available. Seek advice over the radio regarding any medication and how to administer it.

ALCOHOL WITHDRAWAL

When regular consumption of alcohol is withdrawn from a heavy drinker, symptoms such as restlessness, anxiety, agitation and tremors may be shown. Usually blood pressure increases as well as the heart rate. There is the danger that the sufferer may have hallucinations, be confused and suffer epileptic fits.

TREATMENT

■ Calm the patient and assess the level of his anxiety. If the sufferer is very agitated, give small doses of Diazepam.
■ Encourage the patient to drink plenty of sweetened liquids.

EXTREME HEAT AND COLD

BURNS

Extreme heat causes a localised change in the skin, resulting in reddening of various degrees. Minor burns cause discomfort but can be easily treated (for example sunburn or 'superficial' burns).

With severe burns there is deep tissue damage with formation of blisters, scabs and even charring ('partial thickness' and 'full thickness' burns). In addition, toxins are released into the body which can lead to potentially fatal problems. Complications involved with full thickness burns include shock due to excessive loss of plasma, infection and heat loss due to the removal of protective skin covering.

TREATMENT

- The extent of partial thickness and full thickness burns must be carefully assessed. For this, the Rule of Nines is used to calculate the surface area of the body affected (see Fig 26). A burn affecting more than 10–15% of the body surface may give rise to fatal complications. In this case, outside help should be sought straight away by radio.
- Remove loose clothing and jewellery but do not attempt to remove any items that have stuck to the skin.
- Cool the burn with tepid (not iced) water as soon as possible. If necessary, seawater, can be used. Soak the burn for at least a quarter of an hour. This measure limits the damage and relieves pain.
- If professional medical aid can be expected soon, wounds should be lightly covered to keep them sterile and dry; use a clean, dry dressing or clingfilm (do not wrap). Do not apply creams or greasy substances. Do not burst any blisters as this may cause the wound to become infected.

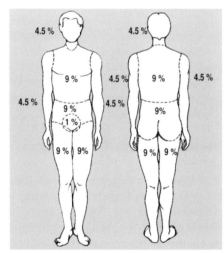

Fig 26 To estimate burn size, you can use the Rule of Nines where the body is divided into areas equalling multiples of nine per cent of the total body surface area. For example, the head and arms are each equal to nine per cent of body surface; each leg is 18 per cent.

■ Keep the patient comfortably warm as there could be a risk of hypothermia. Treat for shock (see page 20)

■ A conscious, alert patient can be given one litre (ca. one quart) of liquid during the first hour, preferably in the form of an electrolyte drink such as Dioralyte (Gatorade). A solution of half a teaspoonful of cooking salt and two teaspoonfuls of sugar in one litre of water can also be used.

■ In addition, administer pain killers; choose the strength according to the severity of pain. Continue giving liquids containing salt; from the second day add less salt and mix in orange juice instead. Check whether the casualty's tetanus vaccination is up to date (see page 82).

SUNBURN

Sunburn is the equivalent of a superficial burn. It is important to use adequate amounts of high-factor sunscreen and wear a hat in order to minimise burning of this kind. The sun's rays are strongest between 9am and 5pm. Be aware that UV light can also penetrate white cotton and water surfaces reflect 100% of the light (green grass, by comparison reflects only 2%). The burning effect is increased by wet skin, air humidity, heat and wind.

TREATMENT

■ Cool the affected area with lukewarm water and treat with aloe vera gel, calamine or aftersun lotion.

HEAT EXHAUSTION

Heat exhaustion occurs when the body's core temperature rises abnormally. The symptoms are heavy sweating, paleness of skin, muscle cramps, feeling faint and nauseous.

TREATMENT

■ Place the sufferer to rest in a cool place, lie down and rehydrate.

HEAT STROKE

This is an advanced form of heat exhaustion where the core temperature rises so high that the key body functions are affected. Symptoms include red, dry skin, headache, disorientation and even hallucinations. Pulse and respiration are rapid and shallow. The body temperature may rise above 40°C (104°F).

TREATMENT

This is a dangerous condition and swift action must be taken:

■ Lie the casualty down in a cool place and remove clothing.

- Cool him using cold, wet compresses on forehead, neck, armpits and groin. Exposure to the wind and using a fan may also help.
- If the patient is conscious and alert, give plenty of liquid such as rehydrating salts, eg Dioralyte.
- Do not give any medicine.
- Treat for shock (see page 20).
- Make radio contact with the doctor.

HYPOTHERMIA: GENERAL

Normal body temperature is 37°C (98.6°F). A person is considered to be hypothermic if their body temperature is less than 35°C (95°F).

At a water temperature of 9°C (48.2°F), such as is found in May in temperate waters, after two hours in the water, the chances of survival are only 50%. Indeed, even after a successful rescue, a 'man overboard' victim can still die of hypothermia, due to rapid, excessive chilling in the sea.

TREATMENT

- If any crew members fall overboard, they should be transferred onboard extremely carefully – and in a horizontal position. While they are in the water they can conserve heat by adopting the 'HELP' crouched position where legs and arms are crossed and movement is kept to the minimum. The peripheral body temperature will lower relatively quickly in an attempt to maintain the core body temperature.
- All metabolic activities function at a reduced rate. You must bear this in mind when assessing the state of the rescued person. Rescue and first aid must be carried out very carefully.
- Ensure the person is placed in a warm cabin (see Fig 27). Any disturbance of the potentially unstable circulation may result in the patient's condition worsening. Hypothermic patients are at risk of cardiac instability. Furthermore, what is known as the afterdrop (where cold, peripheral blood flows into the body core when rapid rewarming occurs) represents a further hazard even ending in death during rescue.

MILD HYPOTHERMIA

Symptoms include shivering, pale skin, pulse rate of 60–80 beats per minute, patient partly confused, shows lack of interest, apathy. The core body temperature (measured rectally) is higher than 32°C (89.6°F).

TREATMENT

- Keep monitoring the core body temperature, as a drop is likely. The individual must be dressed in dry clothes and wrapped in warm blankets.

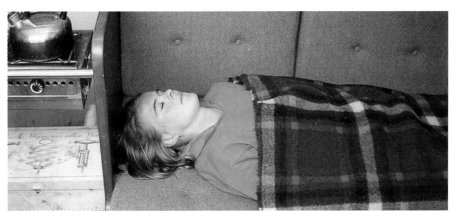

Fig 27 Transfer the hypothermic patient carefully to a warm cabin.

■ Warm the cabin temperature and give hot drinks. The patient should be given plenty of rest. A mildly hypothermic casualty can be actively re-warmed – ie administer warm drinks, warm (40°C, 104°F) bath, as long as they are fully conscious and not left alone.

SEVERE HYPOTHERMIA

Generally the casualty stops shivering. The skin is a patchy blue, in parts swollen and doughy. The condition of the individual varies between lethargic and unconscious, at times agitated, and they may behave erratically and have hallucinations. The pupils are enlarged; pulse and respiration are extremely slow. In addition, frostbite may have also occurred. The core body temperature is below 32°C (89.6°F).

TREATMENT _____

■ Handle the patient very carefully as they are at risk from cardiac arrest. Warm the casualty by covering them with sleeping bags or other insulating items such as fleeces, blankets etc.

■ A casualty who is severely hypothermic (with a core temperature less than 32°C) must be re-warmed slowly and passively. Do not immerse in a hot bath or use direct heat. Do not give anything by mouth to a severely hypothermic casualty who is semi-conscious. Generally speaking, the more severe the hypothermia, the more slowly and carefully they should be rewarmed.

■ Monitor pulse and respiration constantly because there is a risk of cardio-pulmonary collapse resulting in the need for resuscitation as per the ABC rule (see page 10).

Fig 28 If hypothermia is severe, remove wet clothing and use space/insulated blankets and hot water bottles or thermal packs applied only to the groin and underarm area to warm the patient. Give warm, sugary drinks if fully conscious.

■ In very severe cases, where the patient is not generating body heat himself, use thermal packs or hot water bottles of 40°C (104°F) maximum, placed on the chest, in the groin, armpits and nape of the neck (see Fig 28). Do not put heat packs on legs or arms. Take care to avoid burning the casualty: lay a dry towel under the packs.

■ Outside medical aid must definitely be sought. If seawater has been swallowed, there is a danger of fluid accumulating in the lungs and causing secondary drowning (known as pulmonary oedema). This may occur up to 72 hours after immersion.

■ Do not permit a hypothermic casualty to try to warm themselves by exercising. Vigorous rubbing of the skin, drinking alcohol and smoking should not be permitted.

FROSTBITE

In very cold conditions, frostbite may affect the extremities such as the nose, ears, fingers and toes. The initial symptoms are pale skin and numbness. In severe cases the skin may harden and go blue.

TREATMENT

- ■ Take the patient into a warm place and start to rewarm the affected areas as soon as possible. The best way of doing this is to use bowls of room temperature water. This dilates the blood vessels so blood flows back to the affected areas. However it can be very painful so make sure the water is not too hot and, if necessary, give a warm drink with two aspirins or paracetamol.
- ■ Do not try to warm the skin by rubbing or using direct heat as this will damage tissue. If warm water is not available use body heat such as the armpits or lap. Carefully dress the affected area with sterile gauze, between fingers or toes, and monitor on a daily basis.

DROWNING AND NEAR DROWNING

Drowning occurs when water is inhaled which blocks respiration and circulation. There may also be additional injuries such as a head injury caused by a gybing boom or cervical injury caused by diving into shallow water.

The symptoms of a conscious victim are pallor, blue lips, confusion, shivering, shallow, laboured breathing and faint pulse. An unconscious casualty may stop breathing. See also hypothermia (page 28).

TREATMENT

For a conscious victim, place in the recovery position in case they vomit seawater. Once he or she has sufficiently recovered, remove wet clothing and dress in warm items and provide a warm drink. Monitor the individual carefully as there is a risk of secondary drowning where fluid absorbed into the lungs can impair breathing; this can occur up to 72 hours after the incident.

For an unconscious victim follow the ABC rules (see page 10).

- ■ Check respiration, extending the neck to clear the airway.
- ■ If breathing does not start spontaneously, perform CPR without delay.
- ■ Do not try to expel water from the lungs.
- ■ In the event of cardiac arrest, start CPR. Give chest compressions (see page 13, Fig 8) in addition to rescue breathing. At the same time, treat for hypothermia (handle carefully).
- ■ Avoid further heat loss by using blankets etc.
- ■ After the condition has been stabilised, ensure that the casualty is treated in hospital because of the danger of secondary drowning.

WOUNDS

A set of surgical instruments for treating wounds can be carried in sterile conditions on board. A surgical stapler, for example, can be used by a trained member of the crew (see Fig 29).

With all wounds, the patient's tetanus vaccination should be checked (see page 82). Antibiotics should only be used for deep, dirty, infected wounds, and wounds caused by bites. Before you decide on which of the following measures to take, the wound must be closely examined.

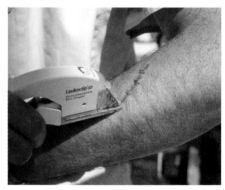

Fig 29 A surgical stapler can be used to close a wound.

CUTS AND LACERATIONS

TREATMENT
■ Clean the wound thoroughly with antiseptic lotion. Examine the area to make sure there are no foreign bodies embedded eg bits of wire from rigging or grit. Stop any bleeding with a sterile pad.
■ Small cuts can be closed with waterproof plasters. Larger cuts should be closed with steristrips (see Fig 30).
■ If the wound is particularly dirty, irrigate the wound with clean running water or saline.
■ For wound closure, Dermabond is a very useful product for 'gluing'

Fig 30 Applying steristrips and a plastic bandage.

together small cuts and facial/scalp wounds, and is particularly good for kids. This should not be used on animal bites, contaminated wounds, ulcers, puncture wounds or areas of high moisture content such as the groin or under the arm. It can be used on certain hand or foot injuries but make sure these areas are kept dry and immobilised with an appropriate splint.

■ Larger, deeper injuries may require a compression bandage (see Fig 31) or may need stitches or staples inserted if the wound is gaping. This procedure is particularly recommended to staunch the flow of blood for head wounds which tend to bleed profusely (see Fig 32). The first aider should be trained to stitch wounds and should practise stitching before the cruise – use strips of foam. With clean, fresh wounds, pull the edges closely together using gentle pressure.

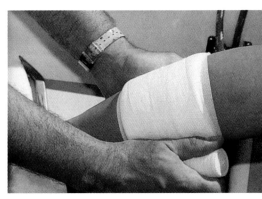

Fig 31 Using a compression bandage to hold sterile dressing pad in place.

■ Suturing onboard should only be undertaken if the first aider is trained in this procedure and only if the wound is clean and the edges of the wound can be neatly aligned.

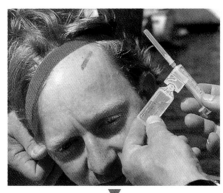

Fig 32 A lacerated head wound being treated with local anaesthetic and stitches.

■ Do not suture if: the wound is dirty or contaminated; the wound is caused by a bite or puncture wound; the wound is more than 6 hours old; the laceration is more than skin-deep; or the skin edges are ragged with loss of tissue.

■ Stitched wounds must be checked daily. At any sign of infection – recognisable by increasing pain, throbbing, swelling, redness, as well as fever – the stitch must be removed. Cover the wound with a clean dressing.

■ Stitches can be removed 4–10 days following insertion, depending on the location and size of wound.

WOUNDS SUSTAINED MORE THAN 6 HOURS PREVIOUSLY, BITES AND KNIFE WOUNDS

In all these cases there is the danger of infection.

■ The wound must be cleaned with antiseptic, and tweezers used to remove old tissue and any foreign bodies. To help relieve pain, local anaesthetic can be injected subcutaneously beforehand (see Fig 33).

■ Old or dirty wounds should be thoroughly irrigated with a dilute antiseptic or saline solution. An antibiotic ointment or cream should be applied and the wound should be covered with a sterile dressing and loosely wrapped with a bandage. A limb can be elevated and immobilised using a sling. Change the dressing and monitor the wound daily for signs of infection.

■ Check the casualty's tetanus status is up to date.

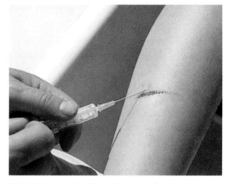

Fig 33 Injecting local anaesthetic subcutaneously to relieve pain prior to wound cleansing.

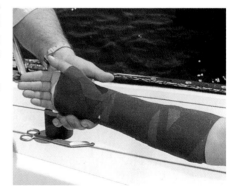

Fig 34 Immobilising a wounded limb using a splint and bandage.

HAND INJURIES CAUSED BY FISH HOOKS

Injuries caused by fish hooks are a special case. Because they generally affect the hand, they can cause inflammation and even permanent damage to tendons.

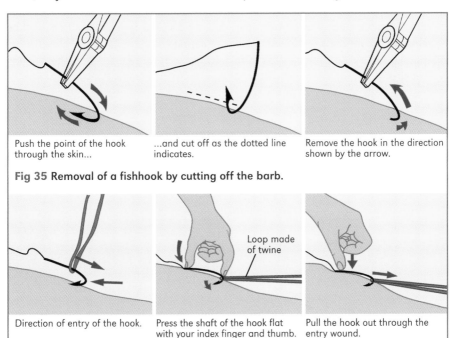

Push the point of the hook through the skin...

...and cut off as the dotted line indicates.

Remove the hook in the direction shown by the arrow.

Fig 35 Removal of a fishhook by cutting off the barb.

Loop made of twine

Direction of entry of the hook.

Press the shaft of the hook flat with your index finger and thumb.

Pull the hook out through the entry wound.

Fig 36 Removal of a fish hook where the hook has not penetrated deeply and can be pulled out using twine.

TREATMENT

- Because of the high risk of infection, the area needs to be treated with an antiseptic solution before removing the hook.
- Give painkillers, and wait for them to take effect.
- There are two methods for removing the hook:
  1) Push the hook completely through and then cut off the barb and retract the hook (see Fig 35).
  2) If the hook has not penetrated too deeply, a piece of twine can be passed round the hook. Press gently down on the eye and pull backwards on the hook; it should come out cleanly (see Fig 36).
- Then immobilise the hand with a splint. Check whether the casualty's tetanus vaccination is up to date (see page 82). If there are signs of infection, administer antibiotics.

SKIN INFECTIONS (WITHOUT PREVIOUS INJURIES)

Skin rashes and infections arise frequently on board but can be guarded against by keeping the skin clean and dry as well as ensuring a good air flow, ie by wearing breathable clothing.

Often members of crew may have existing chronic skin conditions such as eczema, and they will carry the necessary medication to treat any outbreaks. Heat rashes (prickly heat) and rashes caused by irritation from sea water can be treated with calamine lotion or hydrocortisone cream. If impetigo breaks out on board (red oozing sores and blisters), this needs to be treated with antibiotic cream; this complaint is highly contagious.

TREATMENT

- Boils or abcesses on the skin should be treated with hot compresses 3–4 times daily, until the boil comes to a head. If there are general symptoms of illness, also administer antibiotics.
- When you can see an accumulation of yellow pus you can puncture it with a sterile blade or needle; this will lessen pain and speed recovery. Do not try to just squeeze the boil or absess.
- Feel with your fingers to ascertain the right point for another member of crew to lance the boil (see Fig 37). Once the incision has been made, gently press the wound to release the pus.
- Cover with sterile gauze initially so that the pus continues to drain then later apply an antibiotic ointment and sterile dressing pad; monitor the wound daily for any signs of infection.
- Clean and redress the wound daily. If the casualty feels ill and has a temperature greater than 38°C (100.4°F), it may be necessary to administer antibiotics.
- With boils on the head or neck, hot compresses may help but seek medical advice prior to further treatment.

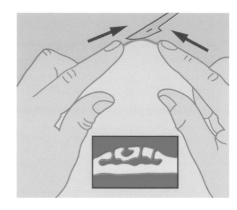

Fig 37 Use your fingers to feel for the right point on the boil for the blade to pierce the skin.

POISONING, BITES AND STINGS

CARBON MONOXIDE POISONING

On board a boat, the main threat of poisoning comes from carbon monoxide, produced as a result of the incomplete combustion of hydrocarbons, for example badly ventilated heaters and exhaust fumes. The gas blocks the body's uptake of oxygen in the bloodstream, causing internal suffocation. The signs are headache, nausea, states of agitation, unconsciousness. This type of poisoning can be fatal.

TREATMENT

■ Remove from the source of the fumes and handle the victim carefully. Give oxygen if available, as the oxygen supply to the heart, brain and other vital organs will have been badly affected. In the event of respiratory or cardiac arrest, follow the ABC Rule and start CPR if necessary (see page 10).

POISONING CAUSED BY INGESTION OF GASOLINE AND CLEANING PRODUCTS

TREATMENT

■ If a crew member swallows paraffin, diesel, gas, turpentine or paint remover, ensure they drink plenty of water or milk. If you induce vomiting there is the danger that the vomit can enter the airways, which can damage the lungs and possibly cause suffocation. You should only try to induce vomiting if large quantities of poisonous substances have been swallowed and the suspected poison is not corrosive. However, the casualty must be totally conscious.

■ In the case of detergents, acids or cleaning products, give the casualty plenty of water to drink. Always try to identify the toxic substance precisely.

■ Some products are toxic to the skin and can cause localised burns if accidentally spilt, which will need treating. Always wear protective clothing, gloves and eyewear when working with chemicals.

■ Get urgent medical advice. Get urgent medical advice. Contact the American Association of Poison Control Centers for specific treatment advice. (See Useful Addresses page 9).

BITES AND STINGS

TREATMENT

- In these cases, the general rules for the treatment of wounds apply (see page 32). If the insect sting is visible, remove carefully with tweezers.
- Clean the bite or sting and cover with a sterile bandage.
- The wound may be painful and cause swelling and/or itching, so an application of calamine lotion, a hydrocortisone cream or an antihistamine cream such as Benadryl (diphenhydramine) should give relief.
- Check if the patient's tetanus shots are up-to-date (see page 82).

TICK BITES

Tick bites are rarely painful and are only noticed when the skin is examined closely.

TREATMENT

- The tick and its biting mouthparts need to be removed carefully and completely. This is best done with fine tweezers but can be done with clean fingernails if necessary. Then the bite should be disinfected.
- If, despite this, a local infection with a progressively larger, circular, red area appears, administer antibiotics. If you are ashore, get a doctor to examine it and arrange for a blood test to be done.

SEVERE ALLERGIC REACTIONS TO INSECT BITES: ANAPHYLAXIS

People affected are usually aware that they may have an allergy and will often carry a kit containing adrenaline (epinephrine HCl) which is administered by injection.

TREATMENT

- Follow the adrenaline instructions carefully and assist the casualty to take their medication immediately if they are showing signs of a severe reaction, for example, breathing difficulties and swelling of face, neck, mouth, tongue, rash.
- If the casualty loses consciousness, assess ABC status and be prepared to start CPR (see page 10). Seek urgent medical help.

INJURIES CAUSED BY SEA ANIMALS

Injuries of this kind need special treatment. They are usually caused by accident as poisonous sea creatures are generally not aggressive. The poison in most cases is heat-sensitive so repeated bathing with hot water may reduce its effects. Take care and wear gloves when handling the injured skin: there is a danger that the poison may be transferred to the first aider. The pain from injuries caused by sea creatures can be very intense.

Jellyfish and polyps have stinging cells which contain a coiled-up thread with barbs in a poisonous liquid. If you touch the cell, the barbed thread is ejected like a harpoon and penetrates the skin. This is why during treatment you should not squeeze the injured spot. Even dead specimens washed ashore should be considered poisonous. The pain can be severe, ebbing and suddenly returning. The creatures can be found on mooring posts, etc.

TREATMENT

■ Bathe the affected part with vinegar followed by cortisone cream. In the event of an allergic reaction (see page 38) you may need to treat for shock (see page 20) and use resuscitation techniques (see page 10).

■ Injuries from coral tend to get infected; they should be treated according to the instructions for wound treatment (see page 32). The affected areas should be rinsed with sea water, or better with alcohol or vinegar to neutralise the toxins. Only then can the foreign matter be carefully removed with tweezers. You can also try using shaving foam and scrape with a blunt knife. Injuries from coral go very deep and should be suitably cleaned with an antiseptic.

■ Injuries from poisonous fish such as stingrays, lesser and greater weever fish, such as are found in the Mediterranean, subtropical and tropical waters, cause excruciating pain and even allergic reactions and shock. In such cases follow the procedure for shock (page 20), resuscitation (page 10) and allergy treatment (page 38). Because the toxins are heat-sensitive, it is recommended that you submerge the affected parts in hot water (only for a short time to avoid scalds). This procedure can be repeated if the pain recurs.

■ If available, a local anaesthetic should be injected subcutaneously in the affected skin areas.

■ Injuries caused by sea urchins result in wounds which are very difficult to heal. The remaining spines must be completely removed; this is best done about five minutes after giving a subcutaneous injection of local anaesthetic to the affected areas (see Fig 33 page 34) – you must wait until it takes effect. Soaking the foot in vinegar can help to dissolve spines that are not deeply embedded.

HEALTH HAZARDS ASHORE

When cruising in tropical waters there are various hazards – on and off shore – that should be considered:

Water supplies

Filter and treat all water that you take on board with water purification tablets to avoid infection and parasites. When ashore, drink only sealed bottled water or canned drinks and avoid ice in drinks.

Vegetables

You take a risk if you eat salad in cafés and restaurants as the water used to wash the vegetables may be contaminated. Rinse all vegetables shoreside in a weak solution of chlorine bleach and take them onboard in a clean bucket; discard all cardboard boxes or other packaging in case it contains insects such as cockroaches, weevils and spiders.

Mosquitoes and flies

Out on the water, mosquitoes are rarely a problem but when you are in harbour or go ashore then you need to take precautions (see also Malaria page 82). Fit mosquito nets over the bunks and flyscreens over the hatchways. Small biting flies can be a real nuisance in the evenings when you are out walking so make sure you are well covered with a good insect repellent. Try to avoid scratching bites as they can easily become infected in the tropics – use an antihistamine cream or a lotion such as Stingeaze which contains a weak solution of ammonia. Some people find that taking a regular dose of vitamin B will deter insect bites.

Ciguatera poisoning

This is a toxin that accumulates in the bodies of reef fish, which eat algae growing on coral. It is not discernible in the fish, either from appearance or taste. The poison causes vomiting and diarrhoea and, although not usually fatal, medical help is needed. The poison builds up along the food chain so it will be in its higher concentration in larger fish. So be careful where you buy fish. Non-reef fish caught out to sea are regarded as fairly safe.

Marine animals

There are a number of fish and marine invertebrates, such as jellyfish, which are venomous so take precautions when swimming or paddling and avoid touching any unknown marine animals.

Hookworm

Always wear shoes when going ashore to avoid picking up the parasitic worm, which can burrow into feet and travel into the bloodstream to the heart and lungs and to the intestines. It causes debilitating diarrhoea, cramps and tiredness due to anaemia.

Insects and snakes

When exploring in the tropics be careful about disturbing insects and snakes in vegetation. Wear sensible clothes, especially sturdy footwear.

INJURIES TO THE CHEST

Injuries to the chest, because of the sensitivity of the pleura (a membrane surrounding the lungs), are extremely painful and cause the casualty's breathing to become shallow. The lung itself is separated from the chest and the diaphragm by the pleural cavity. Muscle activity when breathing in causes the lung to fill with air.

PNEUMOTHORAX (AIR IN THE MEMBRANE SURROUNDING THE LUNGS)

If air enters the pleural cavity via the airway or an injury to the chest, then this may cause a pneumothorax, which can result in a collapsed lung. The casualty will complain of a sudden pain on one side of the chest, and will have difficulty breathing. If you listen to the lung, the sound of breathing is weak compared with that on the opposite side. Respiration and pulse are often rapid. Depending on the severity of the pneumothorax, the casualty may have pale skin and a blue tinge round his lips and mouth (cyanosis) due to lack of oxygen in the bloodstream.

TREATMENT
- If the pneumothorax is caused by a penetrating chest injury and a wound is present, apply pressure to the wound to stop bleeding then cover with an airtight valve dressing that is taped on 3 sides.
- Monitor the patient's circulation. Place him in an upright position and check pulse and breathing. Make radio contact with the doctor (see page 88).
- If the situation worsens and the pneumothorax becomes a tension pneumothorax (ie where the pleural cavity gradually fills with air, putting pressure on the heart and aorta), then needle decompression by inserting a needle above the 3rd or 4th rib may save a life. Whether this condition is recognisable and feasible under conditions on board is questionable and should only be carried out by an expert or in an extreme case under the direction of a doctor via the radio.

THORACIC INJURIES (BETWEEN THE HEAD AND THE ABDOMEN)

Since essential organs such as the lungs, possibly the spleen, etc are involved, thoracic injuries can be very dangerous. For this reason, if at all possible, outside help should be sought.

TREATMENT

■ Treat for shock (see page 20) and follow the ABC rule (page 10). The individual should be placed with the torso raised. An external injury should be covered with a pad held in place with sticking plaster (see Fig 38). Monitor pulse and rate of respiration.

BROKEN RIB

This is a painful condition but in general is not dangerous. A localised tenderness or pain along the rib is typical and is easily felt with a finger. The pain is worse on deep breathing or coughing. All the same, you should listen to the lungs, and the danger of injury to abdominal organs (liver, spleen) should be taken into consideration.

TREATMENT

■ Administer plenty of painkillers. Paracetamol can be used for mild to moderate pain. A slightly stronger combination such as Paracetamol (Tylenol) with Codeine can be used for moderate to severe pain, or an anti-inflammatory such as Ibuprofen can be given if the casualty does not have any contraindications (bleeding disorders, asthma, etc).

■ Pain can be reduced by putting the arm on the affected side in an elevated sling. The discomfort should abate within the next 10–14 days.

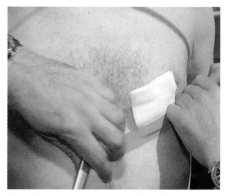

Fig 38 Applying a plaster bandage for a chest injury.

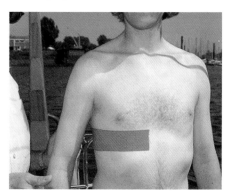

Fig 39 Taping the thorax for a broken rib.

Fig 40 Keep the torso raised to overcome shortness of breath.

Fig 41 Immobilising an injured shoulder with shirt and sailmaker's needle.

BRUISING OF THE CHEST WITHOUT RIB INJURIES

This can produce intense discomfort. Always check pulse, breathing and chest movements.

PNEUMONIA

The patient will feel very ill. Frequently, bronchitis has preceded the illness, especially if the patient is a long-term smoker. The temperature rises to over 39°C (102.2°F). There may be shivering and sometimes a stabbing pain on one side. The patient may cough up yellow phlegm or rust-coloured sputum.

TREATMENT_____

- If the individual is otherwise healthy, he can be treated with means available on board such as a course of antibiotics for at least 10 days (get medical advice), as well as anti-fever and painkillers such as Paracetamol (Tylenol) with Codeine.
- The sufferer needs complete bed rest and will find it more comfortable to be propped up in bed rather than lying flat.
- Encourage the patient to cough frequently and take deep breaths to fully expand his lungs at regular intervals.
- Ensure that the patient has an adequate fluid intake, if possible 2 litres (ca. 2 quarts) per day. Older people and those with underlying conditions need to consult a doctor immediately.

PAIN IN THE HEART REGION

A pain in the chest is often immediately thought to be a heart attack but it can also be the symptom of a number of quite different disorders including hyperventilation or heartburn (see page 24). A person who suffers from angina pectoris experiences a familiar pain under the breastbone (sternum) and a feeling of tightness in his chest. The pain may radiate to other parts of the body, typically down the left, right or both arms, to the back, neck or jaw. Angina pain typically comes on during exercise, strenuous activity or in moments of stress.

The patient is usually well enough informed about his illness to treat himself with his own medicine, eg nitroglycerin capsules, Nitrolingual spray or tablets under the tongue. If you are helping the person take their angina medication, make sure they are sitting or lying down as these medications can cause the blood pressure to drop suddenly. However there is always the danger of a heart attack for angina sufferers.

HEART ATTACK

An otherwise healthy person can have a heart attack out of the blue. Symptoms are excruciating pain under the breastbone, sometimes extending to the left arm, right arm or both arms, neck, jaw and upper abdomen or back. There may be a feeling of tightness and pressure in the chest. A heart attack can sometimes feel like a bad case of indigestion. The skin is frequently clammy and pale, pulse may be irregular and the respiration rate may be increased.

TREATMENT

- Due to the danger of a sudden cardiac arrhythmia, you should get in contact urgently with a doctor (see page 88) if you suspect a heart attack.
- Make sure the torso is raised, and the patient is sitting or lying in a comfortable upright position and has plenty of fresh air. If you have oxygen onboard and are trained to use it, it should be administered using a face mask to anyone suspected of having a heart attack. An Aspirin 300mg should be chewed and then swallowed. Pain relief may be necessary and medical advice should be sought immediately.
- In the event of cardiac arrest (unconsciousness, not breathing, pulse cannot be felt at the neck), immediately start CPR (see page 10).

FRACTURES, DISLOCATIONS AND SOFT TISSUE INJURIES

A fracture is a broken bone that most commonly occurs as a result of trauma or direct force on the bone. If in doubt, always treat as if a fracture is present.

TREATMENT

The basic treatment principles for all fractures and dislocations are:

- Immobilise the limb with a splint. Splints can be improvised by using any firm, padded material or ready-purpose inflatable. Vacuum splints can also be used. Ensure the splint is in place before the casualty is moved, as this prevents further damage being done, eases pain and reduces the chance of internal bleeding.
- Immobilise the fracture or dislocation in the position you find it or in the position which is most comfortable for the casualty.
- Unnecessary re-positioning of the bone can cause further damage to blood vessels and nerves. However, if the circulation below the fracture is impaired (numbness, tingling, absence of pulse, cool or pale fingers or toes), or if the fracture is severely deformed and cannot be splinted before moving the casualty, it may be necessary to gently straighten the limb using slow, steady traction. Pull the limb away from the body, along the natural alignment, and apply the splint securely before slowly releasing traction. It is not advisable to re-align fractures of joints, ie wrist, elbow, knee.
- Triangular bandages can be used as arm and shoulder slings to immobilise upper body injuries.
- If a broken bone pierces through the skin (open fracture), this creates a wound as well which greatly increases the risk of infection. Bleeding from open fractures needs to be controlled by applying pressure to the edges of the wound without touching the exposed bone. Cover with a sterile dressing. Apply a ring pad or rolled up bandages on both sides of the exposed bone before applying a light bandage. Splint the injury carefully, making sure that there is no pressure over the fracture site. Seek medical advice regarding a course of antibiotics to prevent infection.

For soft tissue injury, ie to muscle (strain) or to ligament (sprain), the standard first aid treatment is **RICE**:

REST: to protect the injured muscle, tendon, ligament or other tissue from further injury.
ICE: use ice bags or cold packs (wrapped in a towel) to provide cold to the injured area. This can provide short-term pain relief and can limit swelling by reducing

blood flow to the injured area. Do not leave ice on an injury for more than 15–20 minutes at a time as longer exposure can damage your skin.

COMPRESSION: to limit swelling (which can slow down healing), and even provide pain relief. An easy way to compress the area of the injury is to wrap an elastic or (ACE) bandage over it. If you feel throbbing, or if the wrap just feels too tight, remove the bandage and re-wrap the area so the bandage is a little looser.

ELEVATION: to reduce swelling. This is most effective when the injured area is raised above the level of the heart. For example, if you injure an ankle, try lying on your bed with your foot propped on one or two pillows.

INJURIES TO THE SHOULDER AND COLLARBONE

Light bruising or muscular strains can be regarded as harmless and can be treated with rest and an anti-inflammatory gel. As always with injuries, check motor activity (pushing against a resistance), sensory perception and whether the pulse is present. If there are any dysfunctions here, outside advice is essential.

TREATMENT————————————————————————

- For suspected soft tissue injuries to the shoulder, immobilise arm on the affected side with an elevated sling with extra padding between the chest and the arm for comfort. The arm can be secured next to the body with an extra bandage.
- Always check for good circulation to fingers on the affected side after applying sling or bandage.
- An ice pack can help to reduce swelling and pain over the affected area.
- Acetaminophen or Ibuprofen may be given for pain relief. Follow dispensing instructions.
- Transport ashore as soon as possible.

Dislocation of the shoulder can occur when the ligaments holding the shoulder joint in place are stretched or torn. It can also re-occur in some people who have previous shoulder injuries. It is a very painful injury and the casualty may be reluctant to move their arm. Immobilise with a supportive sling and bandage, and transport them ashore as soon as possible.

If you are more than 6 hours away from shore side facilities, manipulating the shoulder joint back into its socket may have to be undertaken as a last resort, but only if:

- There is obvious impairment of circulation below the joint – numbness, pale cool fingers, absence of pulse.
- There are no other signs of trauma or fracture to the shoulder or upper arm.

TREATMENT————————————————————————

- Ensure the person is lying down with his feet braced against something solid.
- Slowly pull the arm very gently and with a slowly increasing traction along its

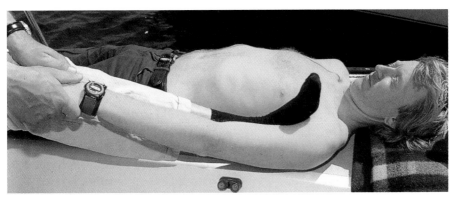

Fig 42 An attempt at repositioning a dislocated shoulder.

length. The first aider jams his heel in the casualty's armpit (use a pillow or other cushioning between the heel and the armpit) to achieve counter-traction.

■ This lever causes the head of the humerus (the ball of the shoulder joint) to spring back into the socket when the arm is brought close to the body.

■ The movement is announced by a clear snapping sound. After this, the arm should be much more easy to move and the pain abate quickly. Immobilise with an arm sling for at least a week.

■ Check for pulse and circulation to the fingers following the procedure.

FRACTURE OF THE COLLARBONE

Fractures of this kind are easily recognised by the up and down piano key positioning of the bones (see Fig 43).The protruding area of bone is extremely painful when moved and will remain so for the first two weeks. Even so, under conditions on a long journey, an operation is not absolutely essential.

TREATMENT _____

■ Immobilise the shoulder with tape or 'rucksack' bandage (see Figs 44 and 45).

■ Seek medical advice especially if there is damage to the nerve or blood vessels.

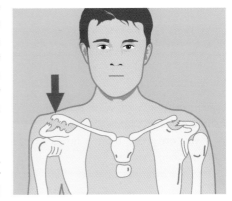

Fig 43 Broken collar bones: 'piano key' phenomenon on the left: shoulder separation on the right.

Fig 44 Tape bandage ...

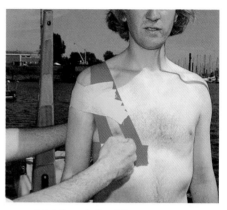

... on the injured shoulder.

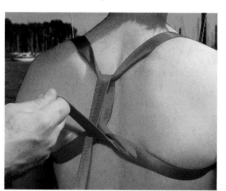

Fig 45 Rucksack bandage.

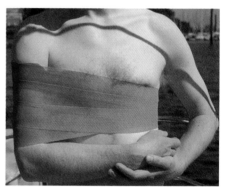

Fig 46 Immobilising the upper arm with self-adhesive bandage.

FRACTURE OF THE UPPER ARM

Signs of this injury are loss of function, grating bones and displaced position. There could possibly be an open fracture too.

TREATMENT

■ Upper arm fractures are best treated by immobilising of the fracture with a 'collar and cuff' sling. Provide pain relief such as Paracetamol and use ice packs to reduce swelling. A self-adhesive bandage can also be used (see Fig 46).

■ Always check for good circulation below the fracture after applying any sling or bandage.

■ Open fractures are much more dangerous as the broken bone protruding through the skin increases the risk of infection. Dirty wounds should be thoroughly irrigated with running water or a dilute disinfectant solution.

FRACTURE OF THE WRIST

TREATMENT _____
- Immobilise with a splint (see Figs 47, 48). Keep the arm raised in a sling and give pain killers as required.
- If the displacement is small, there may be a non-displaced impacted fracture which is therefore stable. Under the conditions on a long passage, treatment can only consist of immobilising the limb with bandaging a splint and sling for 3–4 weeks.
- Always check sensation, colour and temperature of fingers as well as the pulse at the wrist, after applying the sling.

Fig 47 Applying a splint to an injured wrist.

Fig 48 An elasticated bandage is applied in a spiral fashion to hold the splint firmly in place.

FRACTURE OR PARTIAL DISLOCATION OF THE ELBOW JOINT

This injury is common in children.

TREATMENT _____
- A sling is the safest treatment option here. If there is obvious impairment of circulation below the elbow joint (lack of pulse, cold/pale fingers, numbness, tingling in the fingers), the elbow would need to be slowly and very carefully straightened and immobilised with bandages against the torso.

HAND INJURIES

Hand injuries occur frequently and need specialist treatment; there is always the fear of permanent impairment of hand function. Pad and immobilise the hand with a bandage and elevate in a sling. Make sure all jewellery is removed as the hand and fingers will swell.

FRACTURES OF THE FINGERS OR METACARPALS (HAND BONES)

TREATMENT
- Strap the broken finger to the adjacent finger with tape.
- Elevate in a sling.
- Make sure all jewellery is removed.

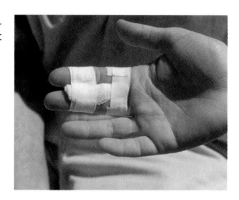

Fig 49 Immobilising a finger using the 'good' adjacent finger as a splint.

AMPUTATED FINGERS AND SOFT TISSUE DAMAGE

The bleeding involved in this situation may seem very alarming, but of all areas, the hand is a part where injuries should not be bandaged too tightly.

TREATMENT
- Apply a sterile bandage with slight pressure. Keep the hand raised.
- Amputated fingers should be wrapped in sterile material and kept in a watertight plastic bag in a container with an ice-water mixture (see Fig 50).
- Remove rings from crushed fingers. Make the skin slippery using soap and pass a little piece of twine under the ring, between ring and finger. By twisting round and round, slowly work the ring off.
- Get to a hospital as quickly as possible, since replacement is only effective within the first hour.

Fig 50 How to preserve an amputated finger during transport.

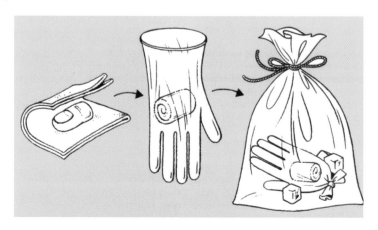

■ Treat for shock (see page 20). Allow no eating or drinking, in order not to interfere with possible use of anaesthetics.

BLEEDING UNDER THE FINGERNAIL OR TOENAIL

TREATMENT _____
If there is heavy bleeding and pain, do the following:

■ Numb the finger/toe by soaking it in ice water for 5–10 minutes.

■ Clean the finger thoroughly with an antiseptic such as iodine (Betadine).

■ Heat the end of a paper clip with a flame to sterilise it. Apply the hot tip to the nail bed until resistance is no longer felt and a hole has been made in the nail bed. Gently squeeze the finger tip to drain the blood from under the nail. The casualty should feel instant relief.

Fig 51 Relieving the pressure from blood under a fingernail.

■ Soak the finger in an antiseptic solution for a further 5 minutes.

■ Apply a sterile bandage and elevate in a sling. Observe carefully for signs of infection as there is a high danger of this.

REPETITIVE STRAIN OF THE HAND AND ELBOW JOINTS (TENNIS ELBOW)

TREATMENT
■ This should be treated with a supporting bandage, either an elastic bandage or a correctly applied tape bandage.

■ Sports ointment (anti-inflammatory gel) can be applied before putting on the bandage.

■ Cold compresses can help to relieve pain.

■ If possible, completely rest the limb.

INJURIES TO THE PELVIS

Signs of this injury are contusions as a result of the accident, as well as considerable pain when the hips are pressed together. There may be blood in the urine. Injuries in this area must be treated very seriously since a considerable amount of blood can be lost.

TREATMENT
■ Aboard the boat, the casualty can only be treated for shock: lay him to rest in the shock position (see page 20) with as little movement as possible, possibly bandaging the pelvis and legs together, to immobilise it to a certain extent.
■ Do not allow the casualty to stand or walk.

FRACTURE OF THE THIGH BONE (FEMUR)
The leg cannot be moved at all, the bone can be seen to be out of position and the injured leg may appear shorter than the other. There is considerable pain. This is a serious fracxture with considerable associated pain. Seek medical advice as soon as possible.

TREATMENT
■ Shock symptoms can be expected as internal bleeding is common. Closely monitor the casualty's pulse and breathing rate.
■ In the event of an open fracture if the wound is contaminated at all, clean it thoroughly by irrigating with sterile water or saline solution. Cover with a sterile dressing and pad around the exposed bone.
■ Before immobilising use slow, powerful traction on the leg, so that it becomes almost straight again. Either immobilise it using the other thigh as a splint (see Fig 52) or applying a pneumatic (inflatable) splint, or alternatively a plastic splint, which is moulded around the limb.
■ As makeshift splints, you can also use boards, paddles, etc, which should be well padded.

Fig 52 Use the other leg as a splint, with padding for a leg injury.

KNEE INJURIES

A direct blow to the kneecap is very painful. Injuries to the meniscus, cruciate and collateral ligaments in most cases are caused by twisting the knee joint, eg getting your lower leg trapped as you climb over the boat's railing.

TREATMENT

■ Cold compresses and an elastic bandage will help (see Fig 53).
■ Complete medical care can only be given in a hospital.
■ Ligament injuries are not very urgent; but you should not wait longer than a couple of weeks for professional treatment.

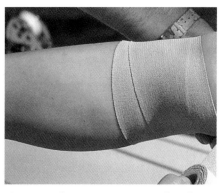

Fig 53 Applying a compression bandage for a soft tissue injury to the knee.

LOWER LEG FRACTURE

This is recognisable by the deformity of the bone. You should feel the edge of the shinbone of the other leg as comparison. Severe crushing of the lower leg can occur between the boat and the pontoon. In the early stages this condition can frequently be underestimated.

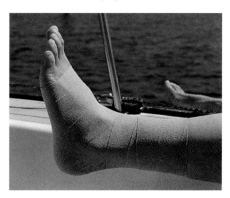

Fig 54 Applying a compression bandage for a soft tissue injury or suspected fracture to the ankle.

TREATMENT

■ Immobilise the leg with a plastic splint (see Fig 55). Keep the limb raised and cool.
■ If necessary, administer Aspirin or Paracetamol (Tylenol). Keep watch on the blood circulation in the foot. Make radio contact with a doctor (see page 88) and consult whether an operation might be necessary.
■ An open fracture should be treated as per open fracture of the femur (see page 32).

INJURIES TO THE ANKLE JOINT

These are usually caused by the ankle being turned over. Without an x-ray it is difficult to determine whether the problem is a ligament injury or a broken bone, although it may help to know that in the case of a broken ankle, there is pain when compressing the ankle joint. With a ligament injury, the most tender part tends to be more below the ankle joint as this is where the main bruising is.

Fig 55 Applying a pre-formed plastic splint for injuries to the ankle joint, lower or upper leg.

TREATMENT

- The current opinion is that ligament injuries can be cured without the need for an operation. Immobilising the ankle with a tape bandage is sufficient. Standard treatment for an ankle sprain would include RICE – Rest, Ice, Compression (with a bandage) and Elevation (see page 45).
- If an ankle fracture is suspected, the joint should be well supported with a compression bandage (see Fig 54) and possibly a splint. Avoid weight-bearing.
- Observe carefully over the next few hours for signs of swelling and subsequent impairment to circulation of the toes. Keep leg elevated on a pillow and loosen and rewrap bandage as necessary.

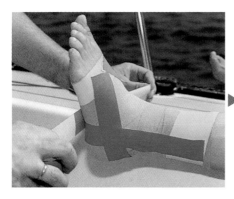

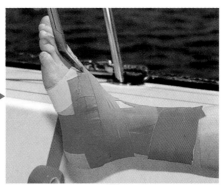

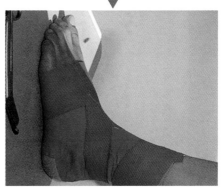

Fig 56 A firmly taped bandage on the ankle joint can provide some support for an Achilles tendon injury.

RUPTURE OF THE ACHILLES TENDON

The patient often experiences a 'snap' in the heel when this injury occurs. You can usually feel a clear indentation along the Achilles' tendon above the heel bone (use a bilateral comparison). Otherwise it may be a rupture of muscle tissue.

TREATMENT _____
- In both cases apply a compression bandage (see Fig 54), possibly reinforced with tape (see Fig 56).
- The current opinion is that an operation on a ruptured Achilles tendon is not essential but a sailor on a long trip must decide whether he continues the journey.

BLEEDING FROM A RUPTURED VARICOSE VEIN

This looks very serious but is generally not dangerous.

TREATMENT _____
- Waste no time; wrap a sterile compression bandage around the leg, starting at the foot.

■ Lie the casualty down and elevate the leg in the first instance. In most cases, the source of the bleeding will close of its own accord over 2 or 3 days.

■ If an older person with heart rhythm disturbance (irregular pulse) has sudden pain in the lower leg accompanied by pallor and possibly even low or absent pulse, the cause might be an arterial embolism. In this case, an operation is required urgently.

■ Make radio contact with a doctor (see page 88)

FRACTURE OF THE HEEL BONE

These can be caused by a fall from an intermediate height. There is considerable pain when the heel is compressed.

TREATMENT_____

■ Urgent hospital treatment is needed. Until then, apply a padded bandage or a splint (see Fig 58).

■ Keep the foot raised.

■ Administer pain killers.

■ Always check for good circulation of the toes after applying the bandage, and be prepared to loosen if necessary.

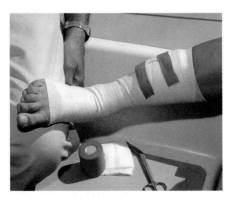

Fig 57 A padded bandage.

Fig 58 A splint held in place with a roller bandage for an injury to the heel.

FRACTURES OR DISLOCATIONS OF THE TOES

These need straightening by traction and then immobilising with a bandage to the neighbouring toe. An operation is generally not necessary unless there is impairment of circulation or severe deformity making it impossible to immobilise.

INJURIES AND ILLNESSES: HEAD TO TOE

The following is a list of common injuries and illnesses. Exceptions are chronic illnesses which are likely to be known to the sufferer.

HEAD INJURIES

All head injuries must be regarded as serious; only the most superficial wounds should be considered as unimportant. The extent of the external injuries is no sure sign of the real dangers a head injury may entail.

External head injuries should be carefully examined straight away. The skull should be examined for signs of a fracture. For bleeding wounds, follow the procedure given on page 32.

After any head injury (eg being hit by the boom), a life-threatening compression (pressure on the brain) caused by bruising, fracture of the skull or brain swelling may occur.

Symptoms of a serious injury are:
- Deteriorating level of consciousness.
- Clear or bloody fluid leaking from ears or nose (possible fracture of base of skull).
- Unconsciousness but, on recovery, the patient remains drowsy, confused or agitated, and their speech possibly impaired.
- Unequal pupil sizes (see Fig 59).
- Irregular breathing, pulse slower than 60 beats per minute (indicating increased pressure on the brain).
- Noticeable physical symptoms such as physical weakness or paralysis.
- Impairment of sensory perception and convulsions.

Fig 59 Unequal pupil size indicating a serious head injury.

- Increasing drowsiness or becoming disorientated, with slurred speech.
- A worsening headache, visual disturbances, double vision.
- Palpable fracture line, possibly with depressed fracture.

TREATMENT

In the immediate aftermath of a casualty sustaining a head injury:

- Sit or lie the casualty down in the most comfortable position. Minimise head movement and support the neck if a skull fracture is suspected.
- Apply direct pressure to a bleeding scalp wound. If there is evidence of a depressed skull pressure, do not apply direct pressure but cover with sterile dressing.
- Monitor casualty continuously – pulse rate, breathing rate and pupil sizes, as well as level of response.
- If the casualty is unconscious, place in recovery position and commence treatment for shock, if necessary (see page 20)
- Call for medical assistance.

CONCUSSION

If none of these symptoms are present and the patient only loses consciousness momentarily at the time of the incident, you should assume that he is suffering from concussion. Nausea and vomiting may ensue and the casualty may complain of a headache over the next few hours or days.

TREATMENT

- Give complete rest for one or two days, observing the casualty very carefully for any deterioration in their symptoms.
- Paracetamol (Tylenol) may be given for mild headache symptoms but Aspirin should be avoided. Severe headaches increasing in intensity, lack of alertness and bouts of nausea are, however, warning signs that severe compression is developing.
- The possibilities of treatment for this situation on board are extremely limited. If there are signs of compression an operation is the only option. Make radio contact with the doctor immediately (see page 88).

BLEEDING HEAD WOUND

TREATMENT

- Head wounds always bleed copiously so immediate steps must be taken to staunch the flow. Apply firm pressure with a bandage and dressing (see Fig 60).

Fig 60 Bandage well to staunch bleeding from a head wound.

- If there is a large, lacerated wound but without further symptoms of a possible brain injury, then you should consider stitching the wound if you are trained to do so (see Fig 61).
- Smaller cuts to the scalp can be closed very well with surgical glue such as Dermabond.

Fig 61 **Stitching a lacerated head wound.**

HEADACHE

Many people frequently suffer from migraine headaches and will self-medicate. Any other minor headaches can be treated with Paracetamol (Tylenol). However, headaches accompanied by fever, vomiting and stiffness of the neck as well as a general feeling of being unwell, in particular in children, could be signs of meningitis.

If the sufferer cannot move his head without effort and shows signs of a rash, the situation should be discussed with the doctor by radio (see page 88)

A sudden, severe headache that appears from nowhere, accompanied by drowsiness or semi-consciousness, might indicate meningorrhagia (bleeding beneath the skull or a bleed in the brain).

TREATMENT

This condition is too serious for treatment on board. Proceed as per the ABC rule and treatment for shock (pages 10 and 20). Make radio contact with a doctor to clarify the situation as soon as possible.

THE EYES

CONJUNCTIVITIS

On board, this is caused in most cases as a result of irritation by wind and grit or possibly a chemical such as chlorine but can be caused by infection (bacterial or viral) or allergy as well.

The inner surface of the eyelids and the white of the eye are red, sticky and watery; the patient cannot bear light, there may be twitching of the eyelids. The person affected may complain of the sensation of having something in their eye.

Infective conjunctivitis is contagious so crew members should be encouraged to wash hands after touching eyes and avoid sharing towels, etc.

TREATMENT

■ Remove contact lenses if worn. Place the patient below deck away from sun and wind.
■ Lay cold compresses on the eyes to relieve discomfort. Apply lubricating eye drops. Gently remove sticky substances from the eye with clean, damp cotton wool. The complaint should slowly start to improve after 24 hours.
■ If the eyes do not improve or become worse after a few days, it may be necessary to give antibiotic/anti-inflammatory eye drops/ointment every 4–6 hours for 2–3 days. Seek medical advice. If necessary give a pain killer such as Paracetamol (Tylenol).
■ Wearing an eye pad over affected the eye can also help to relieve pain.

BACTERIAL INFLAMMATION OF THE EYELIDS (BLEPHARITIS)

This is a condition where there is swelling and reddening of the eyelid. The eyelids may stick together, itch and become crusty with discharge. A stye can occur when the eyelash follicle becomes infected, and is often caused by blepharitis.

TREATMENT

■ Gently clean the eyelids with clean, damp cotton wool soaked in a weak solution of solution of sodium bicarbonate (one teaspoonful in a cup of water) if available. For both conditions, hot compresses can be applied to the affected eye 2–3 times a day to ease symptoms.
■ An antibiotic eye ointment will reduce the inflammation in more serious cases.

INJURIES AND CHEMICAL BURNS TO THE EYE

Injuries must be closely inspected. Only foreign bodies which are on the surface of the eye can be dabbed off carefully with a moistened cotton bud, clean handkerchief or dressing, after rolling up the eyelid (see Fig 62). Any suspicion of deeper injury requires specialist treatment. Do not apply ointments.

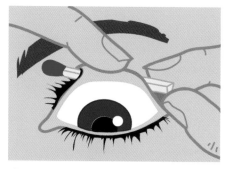

Fig 62 Rolling back the upper lid to remove a foreign body from the eye.

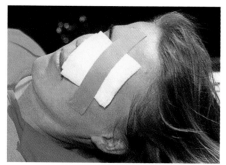

Fig 63 Applying an eye pad with a bandage will immobilise the eye.

Fig 64 If a chemical has splashed into the eye, it must be flushed out with copious quantities of cool water without delay. The longer the chemical stays in contact with the surface of the eye, the greater the damage.

TREATMENT

■ Apply an eye pad with a bandage to immobilise the eye (see Fig 63). Chemical burns to the eye due to cleaning products, solvents, etc require thorough rinsing with clean water (for at least 20 minutes) (see Fig 64). Consult an eye specialist as soon as possible. Antibiotic or anti-inflammatory eye ointment/drops may be required.

■ Any injury to the eye of a more serious nature needs specialist treatment. Even moderate injuries to the eyelids, because of the danger of loss of function as a result of scar tissue, cannot be dealt with properly with the medical equipment available on board.

FRACTURE OF THE NASAL BONE

A fracture of the nose bone is shown, in most cases, by slight bleeding from the nose, swelling and a clearly visible broken position.

TREATMENT

■ Gently press the nostrils together to stop the bleeding (see Fig 65). Use ice wrapped in a cloth to reduce pain and swelling. Get medical advice.

NOSE BLEED

A nose bleed that has not been preceded by an injury can generally be stopped easily.

Fig 65 Tilt the head forward and press the nostrils together for 5–10 minutes to lessen a nose bleed. Repeat as necessary.

TREATMENT

- With the patient seated and head tilted forward, his nostrils should be held pressed closed for 5–10 minutes until the bleeding stops (see Fig 65).
- In older people the source of the bleeding tends to be higher up so that this method does not always work.
- If after 10 minutes you have no success in stopping the bleeding, make radio contact with a doctor (see page 88).

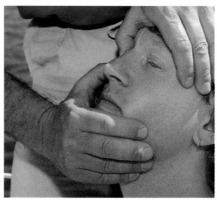

Fig 66 Straightening the nasal bone.

FRACTURED JAW

A broken jaw is in most cases easy to diagnose; even if not badly displaced. If the casualty tries to bite on his thumb, this causes considerable pain in the area of the fracture.

TREATMENT

- Treatment should take place ashore as there may be a risk of breathing or bleeding problems. Until then, ensure airway is clear (see page 10) and adequate pain relief given. An ice pack can be applied for short periods of time to help reduce swelling.
- Ask the casualty to gently support the jaw with a small rolled up towel or pad while transporting ashore. A bandage may also be applied under the chin and over the top of the head but must be easily removable in case the casualty vomits or has breathing difficulties.

Fig 67 A sling for a broken jaw made of webbing.

EARACHE

Earache due to inflammation of the outer ear canal is easy to detect. It is often referred to as 'swimmer's ear' because it can be caused by water getting into the ear, causing a localised inflammation and itching of the outer ear canal. It is much more common in warmer climates.

Inflammation of the middle ear can occur in children and adolescents often after colds. Symptoms include deep, throbbing and stabbing pain, impaired hearing and noises in the ear. Sufferers feel unwell and have a temperature.

TREATMENT_____
- Earache may also be due to build up of wax which is treatable with over the counter drops or drops of warmed vegetable oil.
- The ear must be kept clean and antibiotic eardrops given to ease the inflammation in severe cases.

BURST EARDRUM
A burst eardrum (possibly due to scuba diving or a middle ear infection) will cause hearing loss, vertigo, earache and ringing or buzzing in the ear (tinnitus).

TREATMENT_____
- In most cases the eardrum will heal itself within 6–8 weeks. Ear pain normally subsides after perforation has occurred, and pain relief is not normally required.
- Advise casualty to keep ear as clean and dry as possible. Use cotton wool to keep water out during showering and avoid swimming until ear is fully healed or has been checked by a doctor.

TOOTH CAVITIES

TREATMENT_____
- In the event of toothache on board, if examination reveals a hole in a tooth, effective pain relief can be achieved by filling the hole with cotton wool soaked in oil of cloves. Even sucking a clove brings effective pain relief.
- A definite hole can also be filled with Cavit, a temporary filling. Follow the instructions on the patient information leaflet. It is a good idea to make sure that a dental first aid kit for travelers such as Dentanurse is carried on board to temporarily fix any dental emergencies that may arise.
- If, as well as toothache, the patient shows symptoms such as fever, a swollen cheek and generally feels unwell, then there is likely to be infection which needs treatment by antibiotics as well as painkillers. Make radio contact with a doctor (see page 88).

INJURIES TO TEETH
Injuries to teeth on board must be checked carefully. If the tip of the tooth is broken off, then you must see if the pulp, a small red area, is visible at the fracture. If this is the case, seek medical advice to avoid infection and damage to root and nerve. If

the broken surface is pure white, in other words the pulp is not exposed, treatment can be postponed.

If a tooth becomes loose as a result of an injury, the chances of keeping it are good.

TREATMENT

- Straighten the tooth very carefully; you could try fixing it in place with sugar-free chewing gum or similar. Doing this increases the chances of the tooth healing normally.
- A tooth which has been knocked out completely can possibly still be replaced in the socket (make sure it is clean and the correct way round – and do not touch the root) and retained as it may grow back in place. Obviously it is better if a dentist does this but if you are out to sea with no chance of professional help it is worth a try.

SORE THROAT

Sore throats are frequently an early symptom of a feverish cold or similar illnesses. The painful inflammation at the back of the throat is caused by bacterial or viral infection.

TREATMENT

- Relief can be gained by gargling with salt water, lemon tea, honey and water, etc.
- If the tonsils are covered with small, ulcerous spots and the patient has a temperature and a general malaise, or the neck lymph nodes are swollen, then antibiotics should be given for 7 days. Consult with a medic (if possible) prior to giving medication. These flu-like cold symptoms can be treated with Acetaminophen or Aspirin.
- Eat cool, soft foods and drink plenty of cool or warm liquids. A comforting on-board remedy consists of a mixture of $1/3$ lemon juice, $1/3$ rum and $1/3$ honey, taken warm.

SPINAL INJURIES

A violent blow caused, for instance, by a fall from the mast or a hatch cover closing against the neck could cause a severe spinal injury with possible fracture and nerve damage. In a situation like this, the patient should be handled gently to avoid further injuries.

TREATMENT

- First, make a careful overall examination. You should check whether the individual can move his arms and legs of his own accord (see Fig 68) and can feel being touched. Complaints of sudden numbness, 'pins and needles' or weakness in the arms and legs is a sure sign of neurological damage.

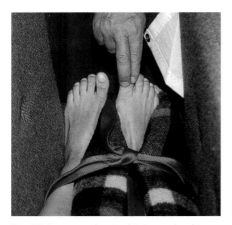

Fig 68 Suspected spinal injury: checking for numbness and ability to move toes.

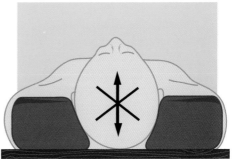

Fig 69 Immobilise the cervical spine if a fracture is suspected; do not turn the head or bend the neck.

■ The casualty should be left in the position you found him in, until rescue measures have been carefully prepared. Do not try to manipulate the limbs. The casualty should then be transported as rigidly as possible – do not let parts of the body sag.

■ He or she should be placed on a firm surface and secured by cushions and other materials for support (see Fig 69); check for numbness and muscle function (see Fig 68).

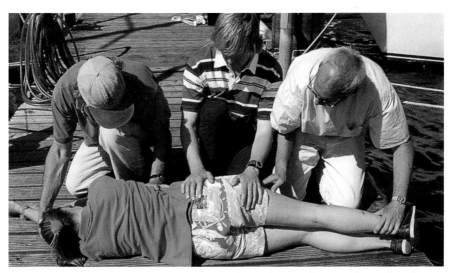

Fig 70 Log-rolling a casualty with a suspected spinal injury, keeping the neck and spine as straight as possible and minimising any movement.

■ If there is any suspicion of injury to the cervical spine, the neck should be stabilised in a neutral position; an appropriately sized collar should be fitted (see Fig 71).

■ An unconscious casualty should be carefully log-rolled into the spinal recovery (or modified HAINES) position which supports the head and neck. Ensure the casualty is breathing normally and that the airway is open and clear (see Fig 70).

■ Follow the procedure for the treatment of shock (see page 20) and if necessary, carry out resuscitation techniques (see page 10).

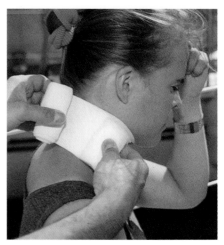

Fig 71 A supporting collar for the neck can be made from an elastic bandage.

■ If immediately after the injury has been sustained, the casualty shows active movements and has full sensation in arms and legs, he should still be monitored at regular intervals since, as time passes, his condition may worsen.

■ If you have the slightest suspicion of spinal injury do not move the casualty if you don't have to. Seek outside help.

CERVICAL SPINE SYNDROME

A painful neck is quite frequent in sailing as a result of the constrained posture of the cervical spine for example, when at the helm. Usually the cervical vertebrae is affected, causing pain to radiate to the back of the head.

TREATMENT

■ Heat treatment is advisable and give painkillers as required; if the neck is very stiff and painful, fit a collar (see Fig 71).

■ Exercises to relax the muscles and stretching exercises can help the condition (pull the shoulders down, stretch the neck for 10 seconds at a time, then relax).

BACK PAIN

Complaints of back pain are quite common among sailors. In competitive sailing the practice of using a trapeze causes considerable stress on the spinal discs. But long-distance sailors, too, are at risk due to cold, dampness, lack of movement and unnatural postures.

TREATMENT
- As a preventive measure, before the sailing season, the back should be strengthened by sports activities, stretching exercises and physio-therapeutic posture training (see pages 86 and 87).
- Correct posture helps the back; it is important to keep the pelvis tilted forward, the torso upright, and the head held high.
- On board it is hard to keep a good posture; just sitting with your head drawn in and rounded shoulders in the cramped cabin can trigger these complaints. The posture of the helmsman on a yacht steered by a tiller is almost ideal.

SCIATICA

The sciatic nerve in the leg runs from the pelvis all the way down to the foot. Compression of the sciatic nerve can cause a severe debilitating pain to shoot down the leg. This can be caused by a slipped disk in the spine.

TREATMENT
- Initially, position the patient comfortably, possibly with legs raised (see Fig 72).
- Anti-inflammatory painkillers, such as Ibuprofen should be administered in sufficient quantity to relax the muscles and ease the pain.
- Too much rest may make sciatica worse so after the acute symptoms have died down, the patient should do some muscle stretching and loosening exercises (see page 86 and 87).

Fig 72 A resting position with the legs raised to treat sciatica.

ABDOMINAL DISORDERS AND INJURIES

An accurate diagnosis of abdominal pain is difficult. If medical aid cannot be reached quickly, the first aider should at least be able to recognise potentially dangerous conditions in the abdominal region, which require urgent attention.

ABDOMINAL TRAUMA WITH SUSPECTED SEVERE INJURIES TO ORGANS (SPLEEN, LIVER, KIDNEY, INTESTINES)

If a crew member falls from the mast or receives a violent blow to the left or right upper abdomen (eg a fall onto the winch crank handle), suspect internal injuries. Indications of this include broken ribs above the abdominal cavity, visible bruises, swelling, pain and they may pass urine containing blood. The casualty may also exhibit signs of shock – cool, pale, clammy skin, rapid pulse, low blood pressure, due to internal bleeding.

Foreign bodies piercing the abdominal wall should be left where they are. Swelling and increased tenderness of the abdominal wall are indications of a potentially serious condition requiring hospital treatment.

TREATMENT

- Carefully undress the injured person and place in a comfortable position in a bunk.
- Quickly assess the extent of the injuries. Carefully feel the abdominal area with warm hands. It may be tender and swollen. The patient may vomit.
- There may be symptoms of shock such as restlessness, rapid, shallow pulse and pale appearance.
- Monitor the pulse rate, breathing rate and skin colour/condition.
- Do not let the casualty eat or drink.
- Radio for medical help and rescue services.

PERITONITIS (INFLAMMATION OF THE LINING OF THE ABDOMEN)

This is a very serious condition which can follow serious illnesses and injuries (eg perforation of the stomach lining, burst perforated appendix or bowel, trauma to the abdomen, ie knife wound, pancreatitis). The peritoneum (inner lining of the abdomen), which is extremely sensitive to pain, becomes inflamed.

If there is a perforated stomach ulcer, then in most cases the patient will have complained of pain in the upper abdomen. In the event of a burst appendix, there will have been pain in the lower right-hand side of the abdomen and the patient avoids any movement of the abdominal wall; the legs are often pulled up. Even the slightest touch with warm hands on the abdominal wall causes them to tense up in a reflex action, or they are already stiff. The abdomen will feel rigid and board-like. The patient's tongue is dry, he looks extremely weak and is feverish.

TREATMENT
- Give no food and only tiny sips of water; call for medical assistance and the rescue services.
- Antibiotics and pain killers, ideally by intramuscular injection, will be required. Act on medical advice regarding specific treatment. Always check for allergies.

APPENDICITIS

The well-known pain in the lower right-hand side of the abdomen in most cases means that appendicitis is well advanced.

In most cases the symptoms follow a typical sequence:
- They begin with a sudden, unexplained pain around the navel when the patient hitherto has felt perfectly well.
- The patient feels nauseous, possibly vomiting, but rarely has diarrhoea.
- During the next few hours the pain moves to the right lower abdomen.
- Now there is tenderness when touched, and pain when pressure on the abdominal wall is applied and released in the region of the right lower abdomen (rebound tenderness) (see Figs 73 and 74).
- The body temperature is around 38°C (100.4°F), and both the temperature and pulse rate will rise as the inflammation increases.

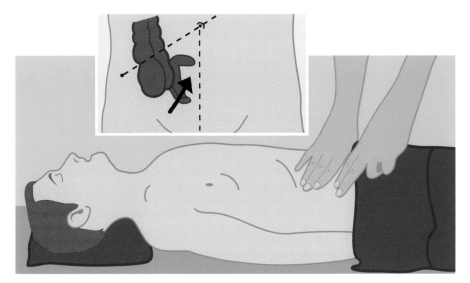

Fig 73 The position of the appendix and how to feel for tenderness in the case of appendicitis.

Fig 74 Checking for rebound tenderness in the abdomen in the case of suspected appendicitis.

TREATMENT
■ Make the patient as comfortable as possible; give no food or drink and lay an icepack (wrapped in a towel) on the right lower abdomen.
■ Contact a doctor and rescue services urgently. If there is no prospect of medical aid within 24 hours, antibiotics can be given, if possible by intramuscular injection.

INTERNAL BLEEDING
Vomiting of red blood or blood that looks like coffee grounds, as well as black tarry-looking stools, are indications of bleeding in the digestive tract. This situation must be considered dangerous and requires urgent medical aid.

TREATMENT
■ If shock symptoms such as restlessness, paleness, or rapid, shallow pulse also appear, the patient must be hospitalised urgently. Give nothing to eat or drink; calm the patient.

ILEUS (INTESTINAL OBSTRUCTION)
In most cases, a stomach operation has preceded the problem or there is a hernia (loop of intestine trapped outside its normal position). The abdominal wall is taut and bloated, the patient has passed neither stool nor gas for at least 12 hours. The condition may begin suddenly or gradually. As the condition develops, the patient may vomit a brown liquid.

If you press your ear against the abdominal wall you may hear hissing intestinal noises or none at all. Try comparing the sounds with those from a healthy person.

TREATMENT
■ Give nothing to eat or drink and transfer to hospital as soon as possible.

MISCARRIAGE / ECTOPIC PREGNANCY

The majority of miscarriages will occur within the first 12 weeks of pregnancy. A miscarriage is signalled by slight to moderate bleeding with minimal pain. Later on, contraction-like pains in the lower abdomen may occur and clots may be passed.

An ectopic pregnancy is hard even for a doctor to diagnose; it is when a fertilised egg starts to grow outside of the uterus, usually in the fallopian tube. If it ruptures, internal bleeding takes place and can be fatal. Symptoms include unusual aches in the lower abdomen, but also sharp pain may occur. If the fallopian tube ruptures, there may be slight vaginal bleeding and very severe pain.

TREATMENT _____
■ If either condition is suspected, transfer the patient to hospital without delay. Until then, make them comfortable, do not give anything to eat or drink, use the shock position (see page 20).

TESTICULAR TORSION (TWISTING)

This only affects young men. In most cases it occurs spontaneously or as the result of minimal external force – the testicle is twisted and can subsequently die if treatment is not carried out within a few hours.

Symptoms displayed are sudden, acute pain in the testicle, nausea, vomiting. The testicle is swollen and extremely tender.

TREATMENT _____
■ Any men with these symptoms should be transferred to hospital immediately.

STOMACH ULCER, DUODENAL ULCER, GASTRITIS

These conditions can be aggravated in stressful situations, such as heavy weather when offshore sailing. Symptoms include pain and tenderness when pressed in the middle upper abdomen or slightly to the right (see Fig 75). In the case of an ulcer, it is often easy for the sufferer to pinpoint this himself. There is improvement usually after eating. You should watch out for signs of bleeding and peritonitis which can be a sign that the ulcer has perforated the stomach lining (see page 68).

TREATMENT _____
■ Give light bland food, antacids, acid blockers, eg Zantac (Ranitidine). Do not give alcohol and advise not to smoke.

GASTROENTERITIS

This is the inflammation of the stomach and intestinal tract caused by an infection. In the majority of cases, the infection is caused by a virus but more serious cases can

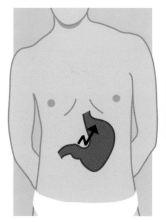

Fig 75 Position of pain to indicate a possible stomach ulcer.

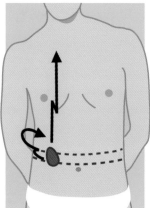

Fig 76 Position to check for gallstone colic.

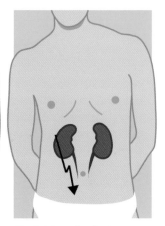

Fig 77 Renal colic is indicated by pain in the lower abdomen – right or left side.

be bacterial in origin. Occasionally, gastroenteritis may result after taking a course of antibiotics.

It is highly infectious and easily passed from one person to another. The infection can also be transmitted through contaminated food or liquid. The main symptoms include diarrhoea, vomiting, stomach cramps, fever and headache.

TREATMENT

- The risk of severe gastroenteritis is dehydration and on board treatment should aim to replace fluid lost through diarrhoea and vomiting.
- Aim to drink a minimum of 2 litres (ca. 2 quarts) of fluid per day. Water, dilute fruit juices and sports drinks are all good. Some people may find that carbonated drinks will help to settle their stomachs. Oral re-hydration salts in sachet form are advised for more severe cases.
- Avoid tea, coffee and alcohol during the acute phase.
- The person may eat if they wish but should stick to light, easily-digestible foods.
- The condition will normally start to improve within 24–48 hours. Antibiotics are not normally required but seek medical advice via the radio if concerned.

FOOD POISONING

Acute food poisoning is caused by bacteria, viruses, parasites and toxins, and is usually the result of contamination of the food itself, inadequate cooking or cross-contamination. Incubation time is between 2 and 6 hours. Symptoms are dizziness, vomiting, diarrhoea and abdominal cramps of varying severity, sometimes accompanied by fever. The duration of the infection is about 1 to 3 days and most forms are highly infectious.

Food bought at markets in southern countries should be cooked; only buy peelable fruit; drink water only after boiling or from original, sealed bottles, where possible with added CO_2 (see page 85).

TREATMENT
- Rehydrate (as advised on previous page). A normal healthy patient will probably recover quite quickly.
- Refrain from eating solids for 24 hours and then introduce a light diet gradually. Avoid alcohol, caffeine and spicy foods.
- Severe symptoms, including painful stomach cramps, can be eased by using Loperamide (Immodium) and Paracetamol (Tylenol).
- Taking antibiotics with these illnesses should be avoided where possible as they can interfere with body's self-healing process.

GALLSTONE COLIC
The sufferer is often aware of the illness. Symptoms include spasmodic type pain in the right upper abdomen with localised tenderness. The rest of the abdomen should permit pressure without pain. The pain may extends to the right shoulder and side and often occurs after eating (see Fig 76). The patient may feel nauseous and vomit.

TREATMENT
- Administer pain killers, eg Paracetamol (Tylenol).
- Give only clear fluids for first 24 hours. Gradually introduce a light, low-fat diet over the next couple of days.
- If feverish, also give antibiotics.
- Transfer to hospital.

RENAL COLIC (KIDNEY PAIN / KIDNEY STONES)
Renal colic refers to the sudden onset of severe pain caused by a stone being passed through the renal system, usually the kidney or ureters.

Inflammation of the kidney is described as colic-like pain in the right or left side of the lower back, extending to the lower abdomen or radiating through to the groin and genital area (see Fig 77). Light taps with the heel of the hand on the side cause considerable pain (see Fig 78). Urine may be cloudy or there may be signs of blood in the urine.

TREATMENT
- Give plenty of water to drink. Any urine that is passed should be strained for evidence of calculi or sediment.

■ Give adequate pain killers, eg Paracetamol (Tylenol). for mild to moderate pain and Codeine for moderate to severe pain. Encourage the patient to walk about if possible.

■ If the symptoms are accompanied by a temperature, this is usually indicative of infection, give bed rest and administer antibiotics.

■ Consult a doctor; the condition is particularly urgent if accompanied by shivering.

Fig 78 Checking for pain in the kidney area.

CYSTITIS

Cystitis is inflammation of the bladder often caused by a bacterial infection. Often pain is felt above the pubic bone. It is more common in women than men. There is a frequent desire to urinate, which will be painful, with a burning sensation. Urine may be cloudy and there may be some blood passed.

TREATMENT

■ Give the sufferer plenty of liquid to drink. Acetaminophen or Ibuprofen can be given to ease abdominal pain and mild fever often associated with cystitis. No alcohol.

■ Cystitis will usually resolve itself within 2–4 days but if the patient continues to have symptoms or is feverish, a short course of antibiotics can be given.

■ Radio for medical advice.

RETENTION OF URINE

This occurs mostly in older men with known enlargement of the prostate gland, frequently after taking alcohol. The sufferer is restless and notes considerable pain above the bladder and an inability to pass urine. On examination, the abdomen will look distended.

TREATMENT

■ For crew members with a previous history of urinary retention, it may be advisable to have a sterile catheter set available on the boat to empty the bladder. Bladder catheterization should be considered as a last resort and only undertaken by a trained crew member or under the guidance of a professional.

■ Other measures that can be undertaken prior to considering catheterization include soaking in a very hot bath, running taps/water and relaxation techniques.

■ To carry out catheterization, ensure the person giving treatment wears sterile

gloves. Wash the head of the penis with soap and inject a lubricant into the urethra.
- Then gently introduce the sterile tip of the catheter into the urethra and advance it slowly until it reaches the bladder.
- Urine should start to flow as soon as the tip of the catheter enters through the bladder sphincter. Once the flow stops, the catheter can be removed.
- Head for the nearest harbour.

SEASICKNESS

Seasickness is a type of motion sickness characterised by feelings of nausea and in extreme cases, vertigo, brought on by the rocking motion of a craft. Peoples' vulnerability to the condition varies greatly but it can be a debilitating condition and especially dangerous if the sufferer has an important role to carry out.

Seasickness is also symptomatic of the hectic times we live in, where nobody allows themselves sufficient time to adapt. It is made worse by working below deck, doing tasks such as cooking and chartwork; symptoms are relieved by lying down.

Seasickness can be actively combated by taking the helm and working on deck. A seasick person becomes gradually apathetic and is in danger on board and must wear a life jacket and a safety harness. The chronically sick who have to take medicine regularly are particularly at risk. There is the danger of loss of fluids which will affect the effectiveness of their medicine.

TREATMENT AND PREPARATION

Seasickness is a misery for sufferers but there are various ways to be prepared:
- Take anti-seasickness remedies one to two hours before boarding:
  - Dramamine
  - Bonine
  - Compazine (25mg suppositories)

Consult your doctor before taking any of these medications since they may cause drowsiness and other side effects. If you are planning a holiday or extended cruise you should try out a remedy on a weekend sail to see if side effects will be a problem. Ask sailing friends what they use. Keep well hydrated. Avoid coffee and other diuretics before the voyage. Avoid eating spicy foods while at sea.

Patches

Scopoderm (scopolamine) patches prescription only. Lasts up to 72 hours. These can cause various side effects so try them out on a short cruise. Consult your doctor if you have any existing medical condition.

Acupressure bands

These work by putting pressure on the acupuncture points on the wrists which then alleviates the seasickness symptoms. Some sailors swear by wrist bands but they do not help everyone, so try them out at sea before embarking on a long cruise (see Fig 79).

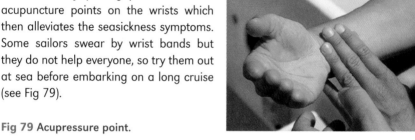

Fig 79 Acupressure point.

PILES (HAEMORRHOIDS)

Haemorrhoids are swollen, inflamed veins in the anus and lower rectum. They can be a chronic condition known to the sufferer or they can be brought on by constipation. On an extended cruise ensure that you take plenty of food high in dietary fibre for regularity of bowel movement. Hydrocortisone cream applied to the affected area should give some relief. Crew members who suffer from haemorrhoids should bring their own usual medicines with them for long trips (suppositories, ointments etc).

DIARRHOEA AND CONSTIPATION

Both these conditions may occur simply as a result of adaptation to new eating and living habits, such as unaccustomed (fatty) food preparation, a change in the sufferer's normal diet or changes in motion (seasickness). But diarrhoea can be a symptom of a more serious condition such as parasites, food poisoning or tropical diseases.

Diarrhoea is when the body produces thin watery stools – usually two or more fluid evacuations of the bowels per day; there may also be abdominal cramps. With constipation, the stools are generally small and hard and the sufferer can go more than four days between evacuations.

TREATMENT
- For constipation, a fibre-rich diet such as wholegrain bread and cereals and fruit generally helps in all cases. Increasing the amount of fluid drunk during the course of the day will also help, fruit juices being especially good.
- Try to avoid taking laxatives but if necessary, use a mild, over-the-counter preparation sparingly, and try to use senna-based products.
- In the event of continued discomfort, it is possible to regulate bowel movements with Metamucil. For constipation: mix 1–2 teaspoonfuls of powder with 400ml liquid per teaspoon.

- Diarrhoea can be a more serious condition. The loss of large amounts of liquid must always be taken seriously. It can quickly lead to debilitating effects on the body (dehydration and fatigue). Plenty of liquids with added sugar and salt are necessary to keep hydrated. Give an electrolyte sports drink (Gatorade) or a simple combination such as cola plus savoury, salty, snacks. Aim to drink about 2 litres (ca. 2 quarts) of fluid in 24 hours if possible.
- Most cases of diarrhoea clear up by themselves within 48 hours but if it persists it may be due to a bacterial infection; give an antibiotic if the condition worsens. Medications containing loperamide (such as Imodium) slow the transit of waste through the gut and reduce the spasms but they should only be used as temporary relief as they may delay the evacuation of bacteria from the bowel.

ACUTE DIARRHOEA
This suddenly affects individual travelers or entire ship's crews, particularly in southern latitudes. Pathogens include coli bacteria, enteroviruses, salmonella, shigella or campylobacteria. The incubation time is between 1 to 14 days.

TREATMENT
- Rehydrate (as given on previous page) with liquids.

AMOEBIC DYSENTERY
Amoebic dysentery is spread through contaminated food and water and is usually found in the tropics. It manifests itself in stools (watery diarrhoea) with blood and mucous. Symptoms include cramps in the stomach or abdomen, and fever. Symptoms may take several weeks or months to show themselves while the amoebic cysts live in the intestine, and are passed in the stool.

TREATMENT
Metronidazole (Flagyl) 800mg 3 times a day for 5 days minimum. Can also be given in suppository form.

STAPHYLOCOCCUS ENTERITIS
This may occur subsequent to treatment with antibiotics, when the antibiotics destroy the natural intestinal flora. Toxin-producing staphylococcus which are unaffected by these antibiotics spread without hindrance in the intestine and give rise to the same symptoms as bacillus dysentery. High fever and profound general malaise may be signs of a bacterial invasion of the tissues and blood circulation.

TREATMENT
- Try to ensure a balance of water and electrolytes are consumed. The sufferer

should rest in bed in isolation, drinking lots of fluids and dehydration salts such as Dioralyte or isotonic/sports drinks (Gatorade). They should stick to a light diet.

■ If there is vomiting, give Metoclopramid (Paspertin). For abdominal cramps give Scopolamin supplement. In the event of fever give Paracetamol tablets or Novalgin. If the fever lasts longer than two days, then Ciprofloxacin (2 x 500mg) should be given for more than 7 days.

■ If there is bloody, mucilaginous diarrhoea, Metamucil may help to reduce bowel irritation. If fever and blood-infused diarrhoea continue even with Ciprofloxacin for longer than 3 days, then Metronidazol is recommended (effective against amoebae and Giardia lamblia (protozoan parasites) as well). Fasting does not promote recovery, but can lead to rapid fatigue. In as far as appetite and vomiting permit, normal food, eg sucrose solution (2 teaspoons per 500ml of water) can be given.

■ Once on land, where appropriate, a medical examination for tropical illnesses should be carried out.

TYPHOID FEVER

Typhoid fever is a serious infection of the intestinal tract and bloodstream caused by the salmonella typhi bacteria. The disease is transmitted by contaminated food and water. The symptoms of a mild infection may last a week or so but can persist for up to two months in more serious cases.

The main symptoms of the first phase are gradually increasing fever up to 40°C (104°F) and headache over a period of 7-10 days. There may also be loss of appetite, sore throat, joint pain, constipation and towards the end of the first phase, the appearance of rose-coloured spots over the lower chest and abdomen (about 20-30% of cases).

During the second phase of the disease, the temperature remains consistently high and the patient may appear to be confused at times or delusional. Abdominal tenderness and diarrhoea (foul-smelling, yellow-green colour) are common symptoms. The liver and spleen may feel enlarged.

TREATMENT
■ Ciprofloxacin 500mg twice daily for 7 days.
■ Left untreated, further complications can ultimately prove fatal.

PARATYPHOID FEVER (ENTERIC FEVERS)

This begins after a short incubation time of 1-4 days in the form of acute traveller's diarrhoea in which the number of evacuations increase over a few days and become blood-infused and watery. Accompanied by increasing abdominal cramps, a dangerous loss of water and electrolytes may occur. The duration of the illness in mild cases is one week, in severe cases 3-6 weeks. Basically, paratyphoid fever is a similar but much less serious version of typhoid fever.

GONORRHOEA

This is a sexually transmitted disease (STD). Two to 14 days after a possible infection, a burning sensation is felt in the urethra, passing water is painful and there is also discharge from the urethra.

TREATMENT
- For 5 days give Doxycycline 100mg twice daily for 7 days or Ciprofloxacin 500mg as a single dose. Seek medical advice.
- Screening should be advised for other STDs such as Chlamydia. Doxycycline is effective against both Gonorrhoea and Chlamydia.

SYPHILIS

Also an STD, symptoms of which include a small hard ulcer appearing at the pathogen's point of entry (penis or vagina), 3–4 weeks after infection. This heals of its own accord even without treatment in roughly 4–8 weeks; however the disease is still present.

TREATMENT
- Correct diagnosis of the disease ashore is urgently required. If there is no prospect of medical aid in the near future, give Doxycycline (100mg) twice daily for 15 days.
- Possible HIV infection acquired at the same time must be considered.

DIABETES / DIABETES MELLITUS

This condition occurs when the pancreas produces too little of the hormone insulin which regulates the sugar levels in the blood; or the body may fail to use insulin effectively. Frequent vomiting, such as that caused by seasickness or serious illness can lead to dehydration and an imbalance in the blood sugar; which could trigger an attack in a known diabetic.

The symptoms of a diabetic attack depend on whether there is too little or too much sugar in the body and may include confusion, slurring of speech, drowsiness, sweating and possibly shaking.

Most diabetics will know the symptoms and causes of an attack, and can self-medicate or tell you what they need. However if they have been working hard on the boat and perhaps have missed essential meals or have suffered from a serious bout of seasickness, the diabetic attack may be severe and so you will need to take action. The patient will probably know whether they are suffering from low or high blood sugar ie if they need sugar or insulin.

TREATMENT

- If the patient is confused and you are unsure, give them a sugary snack or water containing dissolved sugar and monitor their condition. If their condition deteriorates, it is likely they need insulin so seek medical advice over the radio.
- If they become unconscious, place in the recovery position.

HYPOGLYCAEMIA (LOW BLOOD SUGAR)

Vomiting (seasickness) or copious sweating or illness may disrupt the balance and cause a diabetic to have too little sugar in their body. The sick person is clammy/sweaty, tired and drowsy. His behaviour is quite noticeable and can happen suddenly without warning; possibly appears drunk. In most cases the symptoms are well-known to the diabetic so he can help with diagnosis and treatment.

TREATMENT

- If the casualty is conscious, give a cup of water with one tablespoonful of dissolved sugar, a milky sugary drink or a glucose liquid or gel preparation. This should help the diabetic to recover within a few minutes.
- If he falls into a coma, then ensure his airway is clear open and place in a stable recovery position and seek medical advice.

HYPERGLYCAEMIA (HIGH BLOOD SUGAR)

Symptoms are increasing drowsiness becoming comatose. The skin will feel dry and the pulse will usually be within a normal range. The breath may smell musty or sweet. Frequently it is the case that the diabetic has not taken his medicine or injection regularly and the level of sugar has been steadily rising in the bloodstream over the last several hours or even days.

TREATMENT

- Check that the medication that has been taken recently; continue with it and give plenty of liquid.
- If the casualty becomes unconscious, place in the recovery position and monitor closely. Seek medical advice.

PREVENTATIVE HEALTH CARE

There are various measures you can take before setting sail to reduce health risks on board.

CHRONIC ILLNESS

Any person suffering from chronic illness should fully discuss their condition with their doctor, before going to sea, and assess the risk of complications arising. This way, precautions can be taken so that symptoms can be recognised and treated on board. Plus, other crew members can be informed of how a condition might develop and be prepared for it. This particularly applies to psychiatric disorders.

A member of crew with a chronic illness must bring an ample supply of his or her medication and if injections are involved then other crew members should have the skill to administer these if necessary. Make sure that there are written guidelines for treatment in the event of the sufferer becoming unconscious.

Medicines required for chronic illnesses include:
- Cortisone and adrenaline auto-injectors for anaphylaxis (severe allergic reaction)
- Broncho-dilator (asthma)
- Insulin and sugar (diabetes)
- Pilocarpine (glaucoma)
- Anticonvulsants (epilepsy)
- Antipsychotics (mental illness)
- Promethazine (depression)
- Allpurinol (gout)
- Nitrolingual pump spray (angina pectoris)

IMMUNISATION

When going on an extended cruise to the tropics, make sure that you visit your doctor beforehand to ensure that any vaccinations that you already have are up-to-date. Also get advice on the correct immunisation for the countries that you will be visiting. Some immunisation takes time to become effective so do this at least three months before departure.

Vaccinations that you are likely to need when Caribbean cruising are: tetanus, typhoid, hepatitis A and B and diphtheria and polio, if expired. Boosters for all of these vaccinations are advised.

MALARIA

This is an infection caused by a parasite called Plasmodium which is carried by the female of certain species of mosquito, Anopheles. These mosquitoes live in hot, humid areas, particularly where there are swamps in which the insects breed. The World Health Organisation has indicated that malaria is on the increase again, so any country in the tropics can potentially be a malarial area – such as the Pacific islands, South East Asia, Central and South America, Central Africa and even the Eastern Mediterranean.

TREATMENT

■ There is no such thing as the ideal anti-malaria medicine which is 100% effective with no side-effects that can be used anywhere in the world. In some areas there is resistance to some of the older drugs. So each individual has to make a decision as to whether or not to take prophylactic drugs.

■ Consult your doctor before you go for up-to-date advice. If you decide to take anti-malarial drugs you will need to start about a week before departure and anything up to a month after you return home. There is the option of stand-by drugs in the event that malaria is suspected.

■ Once away, you can take preventive measures:
  • Place mosquito nets over bunks and hatches.
  • Use a good mosquito repellent (containing DEET but do an allergy check).
  • Spray accommodation with insecticide.
  • Cover your body adequately after dusk.

Be sure to go for follow up examinations after a trip in the tropics. If during a sailing trip, symptoms such as fever, shivering, light-headedness and diarrhoea have appeared, you should visit a doctor, even if the symptoms have already faded away

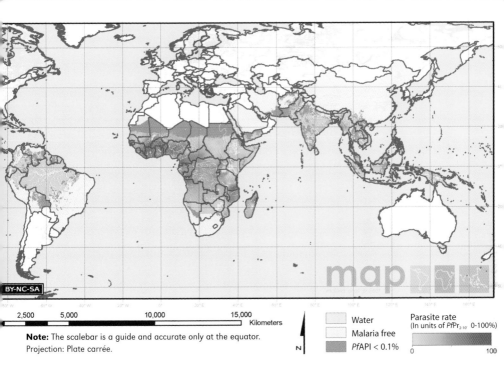

Fig 80 Malarial regions of the world.

Scale: 2,500 — 5,000 — 10,000 — 15,000 Kilometers

Note: The scalebar is a guide and accurate only at the equator.
Projection: Plate carrée.

N

Water
Malaria free
PfAPI < 0.1%

Parasite rate
(In units of PfPr$_{2-10}$ 0-100%)
0 — 100

again. It is particularly important to exclude the possibility of having contracted malaria. Extreme diarrhoea might indicate infection by salmonella, shigella (intestinal bacteria) or by amoebae. Swelling of the lymph nodes or any changes in the skin should also be checked out. After contact with fresh water in tropical zones, there is always the danger of Bilharzia infection (Schistosomiasis).

WELLBEING ON BOARD

NUTRITION

In general, your aim should be to eat a diet rich in fibre. This helps to prevent sluggishness of the bowels which can make you feel very uncomfortable. Wholemeal foodstuffs are recommended, such as wholegrain rice and wholewheat pasta, as well as plenty of fruit and vegetables.

On long trips, take multivitamin tablets regularly.

In southern and subtropical or tropical areas the problem of food hygiene arises so it might be a good idea to avoid 'street food'. The local dishes that you find in restaurants are suited to the country and the climate; generally after a while your body will adapt and tolerate them. It is a matter of common sense what foods to avoid, for example shellfish and reheated stewed meat dishes can be risky. If in doubt, stick to a vegetarian diet when ashore.

Guidelines for safe foodstuffs are listed in the table on the next page. In a nutshell, the motto is: Boil it, peel it, cook it or forget it.

WATER HYGIENE

Preparing drinking water presents another problem. Boiling for five minutes is the safest method. You can also use chlorine-based purifying tablets. Otherwise carbonated drinks are recommended (the seal must be intact).

The hygiene in the ship's water tanks also depends on the climatic zone. The most common method of cleaning is to use a dilute bleach solution (1 litre of Sodium Hypochlorite to 1,000 litres tanks/piping), followed by thorough rinsing and possibly a vinegar rinse if there is a residual odour from the bleach.

When cruising in hot countries, use a colloidal silver based product such as Plation to keep your water tanks clean. Products such as this are available from shops selling yachting supplies or through the internet.

FOOD GUIDELINES TABLE

SAFE

- Well-grilled or well-boiled meat
- Rice, maize, millet, noodles, potatoes (puree), manioc, yams
- Beans, peas, onions, squashes
- Light, or chunky, boiled soups
- Freshly cooked local stew and rice dishes, etc
- Milk powder
- Dry foods: oat flakes, nuts, dried fruit (as long as the origin or method of preparation are acceptable)
- Honey
- Peelable fruit (citrus fruits, banana, mango, pineapple, melon
- Coconuts
- Spices (pepper, salt, chilli, curry)
- Vinegar
- Good quality canned products (as long as they have been stored correctly; beware of bloated or rusty tins). Store in a dry, ventilated place
- Hot drinks requiring boiling (tea, coffee), boiled water
- Bottled drinks (where original seal is intact). Beware, they may have been refilled!
- Cola (also good for diarrhoea), canned drinks (fruit juices)

RISKY

- Red meat (perishes rapidly in heat)
- Poultry (perishes rapidly – may carry salmonella)
- Fish, seafood, mussels
- Shrimps, crab (never eat raw as they can contain liver and lung flukes; fish tapeworm). Only eat if freshly caught and freshly cooked
- Dairy products (cheese, yoghurt, cottage cheese) only eat when made from fresh boiled milk, especially in the case of goats' cheese – danger of brucellosis
- Deep-frozen food (always the danger that low enough temperatures have not been maintained)
- Semi-preserved (vacuum-packed) foods (check use-by date)
- Juices: freshly-squeezed these can provide vitamins and are refreshing but can be contaminated ie diluted with unclean water or fermented. In cheap, tinned orange juice, there are often irritants causing diarrhoea

AVOID

- Raw, cold, stale dishes, raw meat
- Fatty or oily dishes
- Steak tartare, ham, sausage
- Salads (in some countries vegetables are fertilised with human waste and salads may be washed in contaminated water)
- Dishes containing mayonnaise (potato salad)
- Cold buffet dishes
- Duck eggs (salmonella)
- Reheated soups – these are often made to last for days by the addition of more ingredients and reheated
- Reheated food in general
- Temporarily packaged food: dishes that are covered over or packed in plastic bags, etc, to protect them from dirt or insects, are breeding grounds for germs (hothouse effect). If in any doubt, throw away!
- Cold drinks that have been opened or those containing ice-cubes
- Ice-cream; ice-cubes (bacteria, toxins, viruses are not killed by freezing)
- Alcohol: best of all, do without. In any case, the best rule is: during the day, none; in the evenings, only a little!

Exercise 1 Loosening up. Move the arms in a circle forwards and backwards, 10 times each way – when your arms point upwards, stand on tiptoe.

Exercise 2 Stretching the chest muscles. Stand with feet apart and grasp the hatchway. The exercise is done in three parts: with the forearm above shoulder height, at shoulder height and below shoulder height. Push the chest forward each time. You will feel a pulling sensation in the contracted part of the chest muscle. Stretch for 10 seconds and repeat 10 times.

KEEPING FIT

The cramped, tense posture you frequently adopt on board can lead to muscle strain and joint pain. To prevent this, find some time to do some stretching exercises; these relax the mind and tone the body. There is room enough on any large foredeck to exercise. The basic principle consists of moderately tensing the muscles and tendons, and maintaining this for 30 seconds.

You should just be able to feel the tension. Do not bounce. Maintain, slow regular breathing. Try the exercises 1–4 on these two pages.

Exercise 3 Stretching the muscles at the back of the upper thigh. Lie on your back – press one leg flat on the floor, bend the other leg, and grasp the thigh above the knee. Then stretch out the lower leg and hold the position for 10 seconds, then relax. Stretch each thigh 10 times. You should notice a pulling sensation in the contracted muscles of the back of the upper thigh.

Exercise 4 Stretching the thigh extensor muscle, which will loosen the spine. Arch your back like a cat, then let it sag – alternate slowly and regularly. Repeat 10 times.

FATIGUE

On extended cruises, the disruption of the the waking-sleeping rhythm brings with it the danger of fatigue. This is why it is recommended to start watches right from the beginning of a cruise (6 hours in the daytime and at night 3 or 4 hours). This ensures that crew adjust to a new circadian rhythm as soon as possible.

Taking drugs to alleviate fatigue is not advised, as they impair critical judgement especially in challenging situations.

GUIDELINES FOR PREPAREDNESS/ MEDICAL LOGBOOK

You are leaving an environment in which you have ready access to medical care at all levels and entering one which, as well as being removed from that access, exposes you to a higher risk of injury and illness. Ensure that the skipper, or someone else on board, has basic knowledge of first aid and how to handle medical emergencies, assemble a comprehensive medical kit, and collect contact numbers you can use to obtain medical assistance if needed. Make sure you have your insurance identification.

A boat in constant motion offshore creates an environment far more conducive to injury and illness than does a stable platform on land. The crew must be made aware of this fact before sailing, and discuss injury prevention and stress its importance. The motion of the vessel requires a steadying hand at all times. It's uncanny how a wave can roll, yaw, or pitch a boat just when you've left yourself vulnerable. Keep yourself secure by always being aware of the boat's attitude. Look for firm handholds, take careful steps, and keep your center of gravity low.

Nobody should ever use a sea trip as an opportunity to quit smoking, give up drinking alcohol, stop taking anti-anxiety or antidepressant medications, or shake a drug habit. This is a sure prescription for trouble and even disaster.

All crew members should be examined by a physician and a dentist before sailing. The check-ups should take into account musculoskeletal pain, toothaches, cardiac abnormalities, diabetes, skin ailments, allergies, incontinence, phobias, and any other pre-existing conditions. If a condition is revealed that causes you concern, consult with a medical professional and obtain a thorough understanding of the ailment. Ask about its normal course or stages of progression, all symptoms, and what the prescribed medication does. Also, learn about signs that might indicate a worsening of the condition, and what happens when medication is lost or runs out. Make certain that any ongoing conditions are treated before you risk making them worse offshore.

If any member of the crew have a pre-existing condition such as diabetes that requires chronic medication, have recently undergone surgery, or have allergies of any nature, they should, before setting sail, advise their doctor of the sailing agenda, and ask if there is a medical reason to preclude them from taking part. The skipper should also contact the Medic-Alert Foundation (209-668-3333) emergency response service. Once he, and the medical information, are entered in its database, he will be assigned an identification number that will give him access to information about medical conditions and whom to contact should the need arise. You can also obtain a Medic-Alert bracelet or necklace, which conveys important information to providers in the event of an emergency.

Well ahead of the departure date, get advice about vaccination boosters or inoculations that may be required for specific destinations. Before you sail, fill all your prescriptions and obtain prescriptions for refills you will need along the way.

The skipper, and other members of the crew if possible, should become versed in all aspects of first-response medical care. This includes management of an unconscious person, fracture stabilization, minor wound care, and treatment of lacerations and burns, hypothermia, seasickness, dental pain, common eye and ear maladies, near drowning, and chest pains. It is the responsibility of the skipper to take CPR and emergency first aid courses for certification to have at least a basic knowledge in this area. This is the case even if a medical doctor is on board. For those intending to cruise or sail with children, special thought must be devoted to their care as well.

A number of organizations, including some listed below, give information on training classes:

- American Red Cross

- YMCA

- Maritime Medical Access (affiliated with George Washington University)
  Website: www.gwemed.edu/maritime/maritime

- Pacific Maritime Institute
  Website: www.mates.org

- Stonehearth Open Learning Opportunities (SOLO):
  P.O. Box 3150, Conway, NH 03818 USA
  Phone: 1- 603-447-6711
  E-mail: info@soloschools.com
  Website: www.soloschools.com

- The Maritime Institute of Technology and Graduate Studies (MITAGS):
  692 Maritime Boulevard, Linthicum, Maryland 21090
  Toll free: 866- 656-5569
  Fax: 410-859-5181 or 443-989-3206
  Website: www.mitags.org

- The US Coast Guard approved medical training course SALTS (Save A Life at Sea) is offered by a variety of providers around the United States.

THE MEDICAL LOGBOOK

The medical logbook is separate from the primary Ship's Logbook. It is used to keep a record of medical problems of any nature, including illness and injuries of any kind, experienced by any member of the crew. It is also a place to note relevant medical information on everyone aboard.

Columns should be labeled:

- Crew member name
- Pre-existing conditions, allergies, medications, and dosages
- Date
- Illness
- Injury
- Medication given, dosage, and schedule used
- Duration of treatment, and progress.

The Medical Logbook should be kept very carefully and accurately, with no omissions, because the information it contains may be invaluable in the event a condition must be referred to a medical doctor.

The Medical Logbook should also contain a list of all medications kept on board, their expiration dates, and their consumption. This helps you in keeping the medications current and in restocking them periodically.

This logbook is also the ideal place to record emergency numbers of doctors or medical facilities that you would contact in the event of medical necessity.

RESCUE BY HELICOPTER

GENERAL PREPARATIONS
- Call the rescue services on Channel 16.
- Contact a doctor via the radio for medical advice.
- Assign a crew member to keep in constant radio contact with the rescue services and to relay their instructions.
- Give as much information regarding the casualty's condition as possible as well as any changes that occur.

PREPARATION OF THE CASUALTY
- Move the casualty as close to the helicopter pick-up point as the casualty's condition allows.
- Make sure medical report forms are fully completed and signed, noting the time of any medication and treatment given.
- Place all document – passport, seaman's book, medical report – in a waterproof bag for transfer with the casualty.
- Ensure crew members are ready to move the casualty onto the helicopter's stretcher as it is lowered onto the deck.

PREPARATION OF YACHT
- Ensure all loose items are securely tied down or removed from the deck.
- Liaise with rescue services regarding the correct course and speed to maintain.
- Ensure that the yacht is easily identifiable from the air, using flags, orange smoke signals, etc. Keep the engine running.
- Follow instructions step-by-step as given by the rescue services.
- Be careful that the winch wire does not become fouled by any part of the yacht rigging.
- Securely strap the casualty into the helicopter stretcher, ideally wearing a lifejacket.

Photograph: Klaus Andrews, Hamburg

FIRST AID KIT

RECOMMENDED LIST FOR SEAFARERS EMBARKING ON AN EXTENDED JOURNEY

A first aid kit should be modified according to the cruising schedule and the number of crew.

In all cases, certain drugs will only be available on prescription so it is important to discuss your itinerary with your primary care doctor beforehand. Your doctor can also advise on medications and supplies to include in your kit, including stronger painkillers.

All drugs must be securely stowed and it is advisable to keep copies of all prescriptions onboard. Each time a medication is used onboard, it should be entered in a medical log book. The medical log book will keep a record of medical problems of any nature experienced by any member of the crew.

With any medication, it is highly advisable to seek advice from a doctor before use. Where this is not possible, read through the drug information leaflet in the box. Follow instructions carefully, especially in regard to dosage, side effects and contraindications.

Crew members with known ailments, such as asthma, heart conditions, etc, should carry their own medications and prescriptions. Each member should also bring along the names and contact numbers of their doctors and dentists.

MEDICATIONS FOR THE MEDICAL KIT

SKIN AILMENTS

A&D ointment, 4 gm tube—used for chronic skin ulcerations and to prevent nosebleeds

Chiggard—or any one of the liquid products applied topically to treat chigger bites

Furacin cream—used in cases of wounds or burns as an antibacterial

Gyne-lotrimin or suppositories—for vaginal yeast infections

Hydrocortisone cream, 1%—applied as a topical to severely itchy skin

Lanacaine—useful for skin rashes that occur with prolonged saltwater exposure

Povidone—iodine for antiseptic skin cleansing, also used before suturing wounds

Prednisone 20 mg tablets—for severe allergy and sunburn

Silvadene—salve used for fungal infections

Tinactin or Lotrimin creams—for athlete's foot

Triple antibiotic ointment—for external skin infections or burns

GASTROINTESTINAL

Activated charcoal tablets—to absorb toxins

Antihistamines (Benadryl)—for mild seasickness and allergic reactions; also a mild sedative for insomnia

Atropine sulphate—a narcotic used for relaxing the GI tract or urinary bladder in cases of urinary bladder infection; supplied as injectable liquid in individual ampules

Compazine (prochlorperazine) 25 mg—used in cases of severe vomiting to control stomach spasm; also has a tranquilizing effect. This is available as an intramuscular injection or as a suppository. Compazine suppositories are considered by many as the most reliable remedy for the symptoms of seasickness.

Flagyl (metronidazole) tablets 250-500 mg—for intestinal parasitism (giardiasis, amoebiasis)
Fleet enema kits
Gelusil—antacid for treatment of indigestion; available as tablets or liquid.
IPECAC—to induce vomiting in cases of non-corrosive toxins
Lomotil—given to control diarrhea; tablets in blister packs for adults, liquid for children
Metamucil—laxative
Phenergan suppositories—for seasickness
Senokot—a mild laxative
Suppository packets—for more severe constipation
Tagamet tablets—for indigestion or ulcer
Transderm scopolamine patches, 1.5 mg—seasickness preventative medication

ANTIBIOTICS
Bactrim DS—antibiotic used to treat urinary bladder infections; 500mg tablets in bottles of 100
Bicillin AP 500 mg capsules and as a dry powder mixed with diluent—broad spectrum antibiotic, synthetic ampicillin (check for drug allergies before administering)
Cortisporin otic (ear) drops—for external ear infections, like swimmers ear.
Doxycycline—broad-spectrum antibiotic supplied in oral capsules; 100 mg capsules in bottles of 50 capsules
Erythromycin 250mg capsules—great for staphylococcus infections, especially for patients allergic to Penicillin
Neosporine—ophthalmic ointment as antibiotic for eyes

PAIN KILLERS
Cavit—used as a packing for dental cavities
Demerol—used for control of more severe pain; a narcotic given by injection; supplied in 30-cc bottles, 50 mg/cc
Ibuprofen—analgesic, supplied as 200mg tablets
Pontocaine—used to control painful eye injuries
Tylenol #3—to control pain; contains codeine, a narcotic; 30 mg tablets
Valium—also your ace in the hole in cases of hysteria

DEHYDRATION
Gatorade powder—although not strictly a medication, is invaluable as a replacement fluid in cases of heavy perspiration or fluid loss due to nausea or diarrhea
Pedialyte—a powder to be mixed with water to supply electrolytes in cases of heat stress
Sodium chloride enteric-coated pills—to combat losses from heavy perspiration

ANAPHYLACTIC SHOCK
Epinephrine HCl—used as an intramuscular injection in cases of anaphylactic shock such as is seen with insect bites, acute food allergies, or drug reactions

SMALL LACERATIONS
Super glue—holds small cuts closed until they heal
Triple antibiotic ointment

HEART ATTACK KIT
Aspirin 300 mg daily
Lasix (Furosemide)
Lidocaine Monoject 100 mg
Nitroglycerine patches
Oxygen
Percodan
Tenormin, propranolol, or other beta-blocker to control arrhythmias
Contents of this kit are to be used in those with heart disorders demonstrating visible and

unmistakable signs of heart attack. If possible, they should be used while in communication with a medical facility.

Anyone who knowingly sails with a heart condition should have discussed it thoroughly with a physician, and should have the equivalent of this kit along with complete instructions on use of the drugs. Such a crewperson should also bring along a portable defibrillator, and have their head examined before sailing!

SEASICKNESS

The most common of all maladies aboard a seagoing vessel of any kind, seasickness can affect almost anyone. Because at best it impairs and at worst disables, it is a legitimate safety concern. Seasickness preventive measures should begin at least four hours before sailing, and be maintained at recommended intervals.

Compazine, in 25 mg. suppositories (not tablets), is the most effective seasickness remedy. Transderm Scopolamine 1.5 mg patches. These are both prescription medications with potential side effects. For a week at sea, get 10 or 12 dosages of the compazine. The scopolamine patches are renewed every three days.

Non-drowsy dramamine can be used both for prevention and as therapy. Regular dramamine may be preferred to encourage rest.

MISCELLANEOUS ITEMS

Adolphs meat tenderizer (papaya extract)—for jellyfish stings

Household ammonia—for insect stings

Hydrogen peroxide—for cleaning skin wounds, or to induce vomiting

Insect repellent—products containing DEET, such as Cutters, are best

Rubbing alcohol—for cleansing, disinfecting, and mixed two parts to one of white vinegar for swimmer's ear

Tincture of benzoin—to promote adhesion of steristrips and skin dressings

SUPPLIES FOR THE MEDICAL KIT

Ace Bandage Wrap

Bandages—a variety of sizes for small cuts and grazes

Betadine surgical scrub—used to disinfect wounds in preparation for suturing or bandaging

Blades—surgical blades are supplied sealed and sterile. Number 10 blade is best.

Cast liner—padding to put under splints

Cotton—absorbent, sterile

Forceps

Gauze pads—sterile, 4-inch by 4-inch

Intravenous catheters—thin plastic tube with a removable metal component to pierce the skin and vein used to administer intravenous fluids (Experience is warranted in placing an IV catheter.)

Knife—surgical knife

Lactated ringers solution—for intravenous or subcutaneous injection; plastic bags contain one liter of solution.

Needle holder

Resusitube—used in CPR or mouth-to-mouth resuscitation; this device is demonstrated in all CPR courses.

Rib belt—to be used to support the chest in the event of fractured ribs

Scrubbing soap pads

Sphingomanometer—for measuring blood pressure

Steristrips—adhesive tape used instead of sutures to close smaller wounds

Stethoscope

Suture material—3/0 silk with a swaged-on needle in packaged, sterile units

Syringes—used for injecting medications. Plastic syringes are sold pre-packaged with needles attached, usually 3 to 5 ml syringes with a 22 gauge needle.

Thermometers—must include a below-normal-temperature thermometer

Universal arm splint

INDEX